Achieving QTLS

Learning Theory and Classroom Practice

in the Lifelong Learning Sector

Jim Gould

LearningMatters

First published in 2009 by Learning Matters Ltd
Reprinted in 2010

British Library Cataloguing in Publication Data
A CIP record for this book is available from the British Library.

ISBN: 978 1 84445 191 3

Cover design by Topics – The Creative Partnership
Text design by Code 5
Project management by Deer Park Productions, Tavistock, Devon
Typeset by PDQ Typesetting Ltd, Newcastle under Lyme
Printed and bound in Great Britain by Bell & Bain Ltd, Glasgow

Learning Matters
33 Southernhay East
Exeter EX1 1NX
Tel: 01392 215560
info@learningmatters.co.uk
www.learningmatters.co.uk

Mixed Sources
Product group from well-managed
forests and other controlled sources
www.fsc.org Cert no. TT-COC-002769
© 1996 Forest Stewardship Council

Learning Theory and Classroom Practice
in the Lifelong Learning Sector

Contents

Acknowledgements

With thanks to Mary Francis, Donatella Maschio and Jodi Roffey-Barentsen for the reading of drafts and subsequent advice offered.

Every effort has been made to trace copyright holders and to obtain their permission for the use of copyright material. The publisher and the author will gladly receive any information enabling them to rectify any error or omission in subsequent editions.

1
Introduction

If you have picked up this book, in all likelihood you are teaching in or are intending to teach in the lifelong learning sector. What do you/will you teach? Perhaps your subject is motor vehicle studies? If so, do you think that your learners can become effective mechanics without an understanding of the theories behind combustion and electrical circuits? Or maybe you teach accounting? Can your learners become effective accountants without a sound understanding of the theory behind double-entry book- keeping? Possibly you are of a more artistic bent and your chosen subject is music. Do you think your learners can become effective musicians without an understanding of the theory relating to scales and harmonics? The same questions could be asked of just about every subject in the lifelong learning curriculum, but hopefully these three examples are sufficient to make the point – every subject is informed by its own body of theory or knowledge.

This begs the question, can you be an effective teacher and bring about learning in others without an understanding of the theories of learning? You may not think it is necessary, giving examples of teachers who have been doing the job with some success for years without the need for any knowledge or reference to theory at all. You would probably concede, however, that as in any vocation or profession, the most effective practitioners – those who do the job best – understand the theory that underpins their practice. Certainly the current move towards professionalism in teaching in the lifelong learning sector would seem to support this view. According to Tummons (2007, p3), one of the major characteristics of any profession is *a theoretical knowledge on which practical or skill-based activity rests*.

The intention of this book is to help you to look at learning theory as a useful tool which can help you analyse and improve your current practice rather than something in a textbook you have to read to complete an assignment.

The nature of theory

First, a little about the nature of theory itself. Suppose you were shown a particular pen. It is described to you before being passed to you so that you could examine it. You might look at it, sniff it, shake it to see if it rattles, squeeze it; in short, you could get to 'know' the pen by using your various senses. If it was then taken away from you and hidden and you were asked to write a description of this particular pen, it is likely that your description would be reasonably accurate. If there happened to be another 49 people in the room at the same time sharing the same experience, it is also likely that their descriptions would not only be reasonably accurate, but would tally with yours. Any that didn't, could be tested against the original pen and the reasons as to why they were wrong could be clearly identified. The final outcome is that everyone would have a common understanding of this particular pen, which could be verified and agreed upon. When it comes to learning, a repetition of this exercise would encounter several difficulties. Unlike a pen, learning is a process and not a real object – it is abstract as opposed to concrete. Rather than being shown 'learning' and passing it round for examination, you and the other 49 people would have to reflect upon your own experiences of learning in order to arrive at a description. This time, it is highly unlikely that the exercise would produce 50 identical descriptions. There may well be some similarities in the answers given; some may agree, but others may be completely different. Which answer is correct? Unfortunately each answer cannot be tested against the 'real thing' as with the pen. The different positions taken might well be debated and the evidence to support or deny each might be examined but the description ultimately settled on by any one person would be a matter of personal choice and would most likely be that which most closely resembled that individual's own experiences of learning.

Theorists find themselves in a similar situation. Different theorists will have different ideas as to what constitutes learning and different arguments and evidence to support their position. So there is not one theory of learning. There are several, each derived from a different viewpoint. Although we can have one view of a pen and can agree as to what it is, we have several different views on what constitutes learning, each with its own particular merits. These different views arise because we don't all perceive the world in the same way – this is where psychology comes in. It contains different schools of thought, each with a different way of interpreting and understanding the world. Consequently, each has its own view on what learning is and how it takes place. These different views or perspectives on learning will be explored in different chapters of this book along with the implications of each for practice. As there is no single theory which adequately explains all the different facets of learning, you will probably identify different aspects of each in your own teaching as you read through the book.

How does a knowledge of theory help you become a better teacher?

It is not uncommon in normal conversation to make comparisons in order to convey meaning. My new car, for instance, is much more economical than the sports model that I used to have but not nearly as economical as the diesel estate I had prior to that. The new car doesn't correspond exactly to either of the other two but by using them as reference points I can give an indication of its relative performance. Alternatively, I might be describing the behaviour of a group of learners I teach. I may well refer to the terms 'excellent' and 'awful' in my description. It is highly unlikely, however, that the behaviour of the said learners will fit exactly into either the 'excellent' or the 'awful' category – it will be somewhere in between. To identify this in-between position, however, I need the two extremes of 'excellent' and 'awful' as reference points.

Learning is a much more complex affair than either fuel consumption or behaviour and to discuss it in any meaningful way, additional reference points are needed. Two of the theories of learning explored in this book are behaviourism and cognitivism. These might be used as the two reference points within which to locate the learning that is taking place at any given time in a particular teaching session. As with the other examples, it would be highly unusual if this learning fell neatly into the category of either reference point. It would be unusual to see a teaching session that was conducted purely along behaviourist lines or purely along cognitive lines. The characteristics of each type of learning might well be exhibited to different degrees at different points in the entire session. Learning as a whole will lie somewhere in between the two chosen reference points. Those very reference points of 'behaviourism' and 'cognitivism' are needed, however, to help in identifying and explaining more clearly the exact nature of the learning that is taking place.

So what does this tell us about learning theory? Popper (1992) suggests that theories are *nets cast to catch what we call 'the world', to rationalise, to explain and to master it.* Achieving such mastery, however, initially involves simplification and generalisation and so it is important to recognise that theory, by its very nature, rarely provides a complete match with reality. Teaching and learning invariably don't fit neatly into the boxes that theory provides for us. What those boxes do provide, however, are reference points against which you can compare and analyse your practice, leading to a more informed view of what you do and ultimately enabling you to become a more effective teacher.

But practice, not theory, is how you get better

You might argue that the improvement of teaching comes through the 'doing' of it rather than through reading books about it, especially theory books. It is true that teaching is a skill and like any other skill is acquired through practice – but that doesn't mean that theory shouldn't inform this practice. The constant practice of crossing your hands when turning a corner in a car is not that useful to someone who is learning to drive. It would be more useful to practise turning corners by 'feeding' the steering wheel through the hands in the approved driving-test fashion. This would be more likely to happen if the learner driver first understood that this was the most effective way to proceed as it would give more control over the steering wheel. A knowledge of what is deemed to be effective practice and the rationale or theory which lies behind it is therefore essential.

It is useful to look at Kolb's (1984) cycle of experiential learning at this stage. It is represented diagrammatically below:

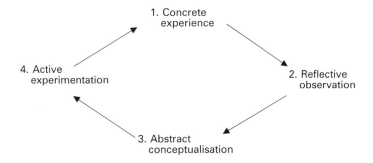

Although the language is somewhat dense, the message it conveys is simple. Kolb maintains that we learn through experience, but only if we process that experience and make sense of it. Experience alone is insufficient to lead to improvement as is suggested by the point of view that *30 years' experience can be one year's experience repeated 29 more times*. Experience is what Usher (1985, p60) describes as *raw material* and as such requires 'processing' before it can lead to real learning. So how can benefit and learning be extracted from experience?

The process of self-evaluation is intended to lead to improved practice. Consider how you might go about this process after a teaching session with a group of learners. The sequence of events might include the following steps.

1. Teach the session. This is Kolb's concrete experience.
2. Afterwards, you re-run the session in your mind: what were the significant features, what went particularly well, what didn't go as well as you had hoped, did anything surprising happen? You are now engaging in what Kolb describes as reflective observation.
3. You then ask the question *Why did that happen?* You would engage in some analysis of the events you had identified in stage 2, looking for the reasons as to why some things went well and others didn't. This is what Kolb calls abstract conceptualisation.
4. The results of this analysis would lead you to some conclusions about how you might do things differently and hopefully more effectively next time. Kolb's term for this is active experimentation.

This process can follow any experience – that first date, a job interview, taking part in some kind of sporting event...the list is endless. But in each case finding the answer to that *why?* question is crucial and often the most difficult part of the process. This is where learning theory comes in. It provides a framework against which to analyse and test out those experiences that take place in a learning environment and leads to the identification of the possible ways in which things might be done differently next time round.

So while experience is a better teacher than books, it is books and the theory they contain which provide the means of learning effectively from these experiences.

Reflective practice

The professional is someone who is continuously developing his or her underpinning knowledge through reflection on their own (and others') practice.
(Gray, Griffin and Nasta, 2000, p25)

The process of experiential learning is an essential component of reflective practice which underlies the training and professional development of teachers. Reflective practice draws on the results of reflection and on analysis of previous experience to inform future actions or practice.

The most well-known advocate of this approach is Donald Schön who published *The reflective practitioner*, his seminal book on the subject, in 1983. Schön suggests that the knowledge we gain from practice in the real world is every bit as useful as that supplied by books and courses. This is not always a conscious process. For example, have you ever dealt with a situation in a way that seemed right at the time, but afterwards you had not been able to satisfactorily explain why you did what you did? If so, you have engaged in what Schön calls knowing-in-action. Your actions were informed by reference to the subconscious store of prior knowledge and experience you have built up through your practice to date. Schön identifies two further types of much more active, conscious reflective practice. Reflection-in-action occurs when you deal with something as it happens, while simultaneously reflecting upon it, thus arriving at a considered response. The process of self-evaluation discussed above is an example of reflection-on-action, Schön's third category of reflective practice.

A knowledge of learning theory informs the last two of these. This is where psychology comes in. The theories we will be exploring in this book are rooted in the field of psychology.

Structure of the book

Chapter 2 starts with a consideration of behaviourism, the perspective that made the first major impact on the way in which teaching and learning are conducted. This perspective interprets the world in terms of externally observable behaviour. The chapter summarises the work of the major behaviourists, identifying their contributions to the teaching and learning debate. Chapter 3 spells out the implications of this perspective for practice within the lifelong learning sector, with particular reference to planning, methods, assessment and classroom management. This pattern is repeated in Chapters 4 and 5, only this time it is the cognitive perspective which is under examination. Rather than interpreting learning in terms of observable behaviour, the cognitive perspective considers learning to be an active mental process which is internal to the learner and so provides a strong contrast to behaviourism. Chapters 6 and 7 concern themselves less with defining learning and more with the nature of learners and the relationships within a learning environment. The humanistic perspective explored in Chapter 6 focuses on 'the person' and presents a student-centred view of learning based on enabling and the process of facilitation. This chapter discusses the assumptions concerning the nature of learners and learning upon which this approach is based. The humanistic theme is extended in Chapter 7, which considers a specific group of learners – adult learners. This chapter explores the assumptions and implications for practice of andragogy, defined by Malcolm Knowles (1990, p54) as *the art and science of helping adults learn*. Returning to cognitive psychology, one standpoint contained within this perspective is that of information processing theory. This approach compares the human mind with a computer in that both take in information, process it in a series of stages, store and retrieve this information and create a response to it. In terms of learning, the important processes arising out of this comparison are those of attention, perception and memory, and these are examined in Chapters 8 and 9.

Each chapter of the book contains a number of opportunities for you to check your understanding and asks you at various times to stop and consider what you have read before continuing. The purpose of these reflective tasks is to encourage you to think about and further develop the ideas you have encountered, leading to a much better 'feel' for and understanding of theories of learning and their relationship to your own professional practice. The intention of the book as a whole is to provide a relatively easily digestible overview of learning theory and the references given at the end of each chapter will allow you to engage in more in-depth study of areas that are of particular interest.

The different types of teaching methods, learning activities and assessment techniques explored within this book have been linked to specific theories. The purpose in doing this is to demonstrate the links between theory and practice; to show how different approaches relate to different views of learning. It is not intended to imply that they are mutually exclusive. The reality is that most teaching sessions will encourage a mix of types of learning and subsequently an accompanying mix of practice.

I am sure you will find some of the ideas and theories you encounter more personally attractive and applicable than others. The book itself is not intended to make judgments on theory – its intention is to inform. The making of judgements is left to you with the ultimate purpose of arriving at your own eclectic theory of learning which works for you and informs your practice. Reading this book may give you new ideas or it may confirm those you already hold, but whichever is the case, those ideas will hopefully be better informed.

Happy reading!

REFERENCES REFERENCES **REFERENCES** REFERENCES REFERENCES REFERENCES

Gray D, Griffin C and Nasta T (2000) *Training to teach in further and adult education.* Cheltenham: Stanley Thornes.

Knowles, M (1990) *The adult learner: a neglected species* (4th edn). Houston: Gulf Publishing Company.

Kolb, D (1984) *Experiential learning: experience as the source of learning and development.* New Jersey: Prentice-Hall.

Popper, K (1992) *The logic of scientific discovery* (revised edn). London & New York: Routledge.

Schön, D (1983) *The reflective practitioner: how professionals think in action*. New York: Basic Books.

Tummons, J (2007) *Becoming a professional tutor in the lifelong learning sector.* Exeter: Learning Matters.

Usher, R (1985) Beyond the anecdotal: adult learning and the use of experience. *Studies in the Education of Adults*, 17(1): 59–75.

2
Behaviourism

Chapter overview and objectives

Different psychological perspectives present markedly different views of learning and the learning process. One such perspective, behaviourism, is the subject of this chapter, which starts by examining the roots of this approach with its emphasis on 'externally observable behaviour'. The work of some of behaviourism's more prominent exponents – Watson, Pavlov, Skinner and Thorndike – is discussed, leading to a definition of learning and a consideration of different aspects of the learning process, such as motivation and transfer of learning.

When you have worked through this chapter you will be able to:

- **identify the rationale behind the behaviourist approach;**
- **discuss the contributions of Watson, Pavlov, Skinner and Thorndike to this perspective on learning;**
- **define learning from a behaviourist perspective;**
- **describe how reasonably complex learning patterns can be built up;**
- **recognise the role that reinforcement plays in establishing learning;**
- **differentiate between reinforcement and punishment;**
- **recognise why transfer is limited in a behaviourist approach to learning.**

This chapter contributes to the following values and areas of professional knowledge as contained in the LLUK professional standards for teachers, tutors and trainers in the lifelong learning sector:

AS4, BS2, CS4, DS3

AK1.1, AK4.1, AK4.3, BK1.1, BK1.2, BK1.3, BK2.1, BK2.7, CK3.1

Background to behaviourism

As the various views on learning that we shall be exploring all stem from psychology, it would be useful to first understand a little about psychology itself, and how these different perspectives contained within it first came to prominence.

People have speculated for thousands of years on how the human mind works. Traditionally this has been the territory of philosophy and many philosophers, over the years, have tried to shed light on this matter by putting forward their own particular theories and ideas. The problem with such theories and ideas, however, is that they cannot really be proved and without proof it is difficult to convince others that what is proposed is actually the case. To convert the doubters some actual physical evidence is required. This then is the dilemma of philosophy. Prolonged and profound thought leads to considered ideas, but these can only really be supported by the logic of debate rather than real physical evidence.

The early 1880s, however, saw a move towards a more structured approach to unravelling the mystery of the mind with the introduction of a technique known as introspection.

Introspection involved looking inward or self-scrutinising. People would be asked to contemplate and describe their own mental processes as they took place and the results would be recorded. This was done in a controlled manner, so that each person experienced exactly the same conditions and circumstances. This attempt to describe and measure what was happening in the mind and its more systematic, scientific approach was responsible for creating an initial distinction between philosophy and the emerging discipline of psychology.

Introspection, however, was not without its problems.

REFLECTIVE TASK

Suppose you go to your local doctor with a severe migraine and he tells you he has found a new treatment for it. You are naturally overjoyed, but then he tells you that the treatment involves boring tiny holes in your head at strategic points. The doctor tells you he has arrived at this new treatment by asking lots of different migraine sufferers to describe to him exactly what was happening in their head when they suffered a migraine attack. The answers they gave and the consistency of their descriptions has convinced him that this new treatment is a winner. Would you be convinced by this new wonder treatment?

If so, why?

If not, why not?

The doctor has used a form of introspection to arrive at his conclusion and I am guessing you were not enthusiastic about his new treatment. Your reasons probably coincide with the objections to introspection or self-scrutiny as a 'scientific' approach. These include the following.

● The subjective nature of the process – only the individual can 'observe' their own mental processes and whatever description they come up with cannot be externally checked or verified. If two individuals give conflicting descriptions, on what basis can a decision be made as to which one is 'right'?
● It is extremely difficult, if not impossible, to accurately describe the processes occurring in their minds.
● Thinking about what is going on in the mind in order to report it to others, interferes with the actual thought processes that are being reported upon.

The American psychologist John B. Watson (1919) was a particularly vocal opponent of introspection. Watson was of the opinion that for psychology to become accepted as a true science, the associated objectivity, precision and rigour required could not be achieved through the study of individual mental processes which are inaccessible to others.

What could be directly observed and directly and accurately measured, however, were the behaviours that people exhibited. These behaviours, according to Watson, indicated how people responded to their environment and the stimuli that it provided. A focus on behaviour then, would allow the making of observations which were free of bias and, most importantly, could be checked and independently verified by others.

Behaviourism then, came about as a response to the previous practice of introspection. Its purpose was to provide a more scientific approach in which the world is interpreted in terms of externally observable behaviour.

Although Watson is largely credited with introducing the idea of Behaviourism, it is Ivan Pavlov (1927) and his famous dogs with whom most people are familiar.

Pavlov, dogs and the language of behaviourism

Pavlov's early work was concerned with the digestion of food. The first stage of digestion occurs in the mouth with the production of saliva, and as part of his studies Pavlov investigated this process of salivation. He used dogs for his experiments, and one of these experiments involved collecting and measuring the amount of saliva produced when either meat powder or food was placed in the dog's mouth. It is important to recognise that the production of saliva under these circumstances is an involuntary or reflex action. It is not a conscious act. The dog does not think about salivating or actively salivate any more than you or I do when our mouth 'waters' when we eat our favourite meal.

In the language of behaviourism, the food is known as the stimulus since it produces or triggers the salivation. The salivation itself is termed the response.

What caught Pavlov's attention, however, was that after this experiment had been repeated a number of times the dog began to salivate before the meat powder or food was placed in its mouth. The sight or smell of the food or even the sight or sound of the person who delivered the food was sufficient to start the dog salivating. Most people would probably have thought nothing of this, but Pavlov was intrigued by what he had noticed and decided to explore this phenomenon further. He conducted a series of experiments whereby he would ring a bell before immediately presenting the dog with food. He found that after he had repeated this procedure a number of times, the bell by itself was sufficient to cause the dog to salivate.

According to Pavlov, the dog had now 'learned' to salivate to the sound of the bell. Learning had taken place because the dog was now exhibiting a form of behaviour it did not exhibit before. If Pavlov went out into the street and rang his bell at any dog that happened to be passing by, this dog would not salivate at the sound of the bell. The original dog has therefore undergone a change in behaviour. This change in behaviour is viewed as a basic kind of learning known as classical conditioning and involves the formation of an association between a stimulus from the environment (the bell) and a given response (salivation).

Because the original salivation was not deliberate, but a natural response to the sensation of food on the tongue it is termed an unconditioned response and the food an unconditioned stimulus as it also is a natural cause of salivation. As far as the dog in the street is concerned, the bell is a neutral stimulus since it does not on its own cause salivation as a response. Prior to learning taking place, the bell is also a neutral stimulus for Pavlov's dog but it becomes a conditioned stimulus when it causes salivation of its own accord. When salivation happens as a result of the bell being rung, it is called the conditioned response.

PRACTICAL TASK PRACTICAL TASK **PRACTICAL TASK** PRACTICAL TASK **PRACTICAL TASK**

Johnny and Jenny are childhood sweethearts. Johnny always gets a warm feeling inside when he sees Jenny. Johnny doesn't particularly like music but Jenny has a favourite song that she always plays on her CD player when Johnny comes round to her house. One day, Johnny is walking down the street when he hears Jenny's favourite song on a passing car radio. Johnny gets a warm feeling inside.

Identify the following in this true love story.

(a) the initial unconditioned stimulus;

(b) the conditioned response;

(c) the neutral stimulus that becomes the conditioned stimulus;

(d) the original unconditioned response.

Check your answers with those at the end of the chapter before reading on.

Returning to Pavlov's dog, it is now evident that the food (unconditioned stimulus) originally led to salivation (unconditioned response) as a reflex action – this is a natural behaviour which already exists in all dogs so cannot be classified as learning. Eventually, however, under the right conditions, the bell (conditioned stimulus) can be made to lead to salivation (now the conditioned response since it is brought about by the bell). This is not a natural behaviour exhibited by all dogs, and therefore Pavlov's dog can be said to have 'learned' this behaviour.

REFLECTIVE TASK

Pavlov has shown how a dog can be made to 'drool' to the sound of a bell, but how can this inform your practice? Can you identify an application of Pavlov's work in your teaching?

So, how does Pavlov inform a view of learning? Initially, he provides the beginnings of a definition:

Learning is a change in behaviour.

This definition can be further extended, however, by a consideration of Watson's views on learning. Watson was of the opinion that everyone possesses a certain number of reflexes and he considered learning to be largely a matter of classical conditioning involving these reflexes. The stimulus that 'triggers' the reflex comes from the environment and so learning can be considered to take place as a result of interactions with the environment, or what is more simply known as 'experience'. Learning then, is a direct consequence of the experiences that people have through direct contact with their environment. Thus the fuller definition of learning that comes from behaviourism is:

Learning is a change in behaviour brought about by some form of action or experience.

A definition of the process that takes place is:

Learning is brought about by the association or pairing of a stimulus with a response.

This is often represented as S–R, the line joining the stimulus (S) and the response (R) representing what is variously termed the 'connection' or 'bond' between them. A specific stimulus will automatically bring about an identical response each time it is presented.

Although the work of Pavlov provides a useful introduction to the nature of learning and the language of behaviourism, Pavlov has limited value in terms of teaching and learning, as classical conditioning pairs a stimulus with a naturally occurring, pre-existing response. The learning that is brought about as a result of teaching invariably involves the forming of 'new' responses.

Pavlov's work does contain a salutary message for all teachers, however, as it can have a major impact on attitudes to learning. The response we make to a person, situation or object that has previously been associated with a pleasant or unpleasant outcome forms a significant part of our emotions and many of our likes, dislikes and emotional reactions are considered to result from classical conditioning. Suppose you are in a crowded lift and it gets stuck between floors for some time. How will you feel when you get into another lift or even an enclosed space of any kind? Suppose you meet a dog for the first time and it licks your hand and is generally playful. Are you liable to like or dislike other dogs you meet in the future? Suppose at school you have a history teacher who is impatient with you and always asks you questions which are too difficult for you. Will you look forward to history lessons? Your geography teacher, on the other hand, is friendly and supportive and praises you when you do well. Will you have the same attitude towards geography as you have towards history?

It can be seen that as well as teaching learners about their subject, teachers also unconsciously teach learners to like or dislike it. Sousa (2006, p44) warns that *how a person 'feels' about a learning situation determines the amount of attention devoted to it.*

Just as advertisers present their products against a background of happy scenes and beautiful scenery in order to promote a positive attitude to whatever they are selling, a similar strategy needs to be employed in the classroom if you wish to see enthusiastic and motivated faces in front of you when you teach. By ensuring that exposure to you and your subject (stimulus) is associated with a good social environment, active, interesting learning activities and a sense of achievement (positive response), you can condition your learners into a positive attitude towards your teaching sessions. Naturally the opposite also applies.

In terms of the practicalities of teaching, however, the work of B. F. Skinner (1953) is far more influential and provides the basis of many of the strategies employed by teachers.

Skinner, rats and operant conditioning

Skinner's most famous experiment involved what has subsequently become known as the 'Skinner box'. In its simplest form this was a cage equipped with a lever and a food dispenser. A rat was placed in the cage. It began to explore its new environment, wandering about the cage, sniffing around and in the process randomly touched different parts of the wall and floor of the cage. In its wanderings it accidentally brushed against the lever which caused a tasty morsel of food to be delivered by the food dispenser. After consuming the food, the rat continued to roam around the cage and eventually again accidentally touched the lever, resulting in another delivery of food. With repetitions of this pattern the rat became less random in its wanderings and more consistent in its lever-pressing behaviour. Eventually, the rat became a confirmed lever presser when introduced into the cage.

The experiment was extended by the introduction of a light wired in such a way that the food dispenser functioned only when the light was switched on. Pressing the lever with the light switched off would not produce food. Under this set of circumstances and with sufficient repetition, the rat established a behaviour pattern which involved pressing the lever only when the light came on. The rat was now exhibiting a change in behaviour and in behavioural terms, learning had therefore taken place. A connection had been formed between the stimulus (light) and the response (pressing the lever).

REFLECTIVE TASK

In what ways does Skinner's work differ from that of Pavlov?

How do the actions of Skinner's rat differ from those of Pavlov's dog?

Are they equally active?

Does Skinner's work open up any new avenues for you as a teacher?

There are a number of important differences between the change in behaviour or learning undergone by Skinner's rat and Pavlov's dog.

In the salivation experiment, the response made by Pavlov's dog was a reflex action and was a reaction to the environment. Skinner's rat, however, acted upon the environment rather than reacting to it and did so in a manner which did not result from a natural reflex. The action was a new behaviour. As Skinner's rat performed an action or 'operated' on its immediate environment, this type of conditioning is known as operant conditioning. When we pick up and answer the telephone on hearing it ring or stop at a red traffic light in our car, we are demonstrating operant conditioning in action. We are acting upon the environment (picking up the telephone, stopping the car) and demonstrating a behaviour that is not a natural reflex action. It would seem then, that operant conditioning constitutes a far more useful form of learning than classical conditioning.

Shaping behaviour

So far the changes in behaviour, or 'learning' discussed, have been of a relatively simple and spontaneous nature. The strategies employed have been either to start with a pre-existing behaviour and pair it with a new stimulus (Pavlov and classical conditioning) or to reinforce a given behaviour as and when it occurs by chance, and in so doing establish a new behaviour pattern (Skinner and operant conditioning).

Suppose you wanted to teach a pet monkey to pick up a piece of litter and put it into the wastepaper basket in the corner of the room. Classical conditioning would not help you to achieve this as the behaviour you are looking for is not a naturally occurring reflex. You could, however, use the principles of operant conditioning. This would involve waiting for the monkey to pick up the litter and put it into the wastepaper basket purely by chance and then immediately reinforcing it. The likelihood of this happening, however, is extremely low and there are a number of associated practical problems. You would undoubtedly lose interest or even die of old age while waiting for this behaviour to occur by chance.

REFLECTIVE TASK

Does this mean that behaviourism can only be used for learning which involves simple or spontaneous behaviours? What do you think? Consider this question in the light of the learning that occurs in your working environment.

According to Skinner (1953, p91), *Operant conditioning shapes behaviour as a sculptor shapes a lump of clay*. The implication is that complex behaviours which are not part of the normal repertoire can be learned through a behaviourist approach. This can only be achieved, however, if they are considered as a series of simpler behaviours which can be fairly easily learned in a sequential manner. Skinner even managed to 'teach' pigeons to play a form of table tennis using specially constructed bats in their beaks. This process is known, as the above quote suggests, as shaping.

In applying this technique to the pet monkey above, you would first of all put the monkey in the room with the piece of paper on the floor and the wastepaper basket in the corner. If the monkey went near to the piece of paper you would reward it with a bit of banana. Eventually the monkey would automatically go towards the piece of paper. You would now no longer reward this behaviour but give the reward of the bit of banana only if the monkey happened to touch the piece of paper. You would next reward the monkey only when it picked up the piece of paper, then when that behaviour pattern was established, only when it picked up the paper and carried it towards the wastepaper basket. The final stages would be touching the wastepaper basket with the piece of paper and then eventually dropping the piece of paper into the basket.

Hergenhahn and Olson (2001, p83) liken this to the childhood game of 'Hot and cold', when the child has to find a hidden object and is told that they are 'cold' when nowhere near the object, 'warm' as they get closer, 'hot' as they get closer still and finally 'red hot' when they are next to the object.

Shaping therefore involves breaking down the desired behaviour into a number of smaller steps and reinforcing these sequentially until eventually the desired behaviour is achieved. The final behaviour we are looking for is known as the terminal behaviour and the different steps reinforced along the way are known as successive approximations.

Complex learning can thus be achieved through a behaviourist approach, but requires breaking down into smaller stages first. As these stages are then achieved in a defined sequence, this type of learning is known as step-by-step learning. This is illustrated in the diagram below as it applies to your now tidy monkey. S1 is the stimulus provided by the surroundings and responses R1 to R6 are the successive approximations required to achieve the terminal behaviour of depositing the piece of paper into the wastepaper basket.

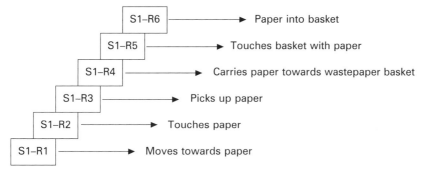

It can now be seen how learning is built up in a behaviourist approach allowing reasonably complex learning to take place.

Learning is built up in a step-by-step fashion.

Reinforcement and the strengthening of responses

Behaviourism generally looks to two different types of explanation as to why learning takes place. Lefrançois (1999, p130) suggests these are *those based on* contiguity *(simultaneity of stimulus and response events) and those based on the* effects *of* behaviour *(reinforcement and punishment).*

Pavlov and Watson were mainly interested in the pairing of a neutral stimulus with an unconditioned stimulus and finding the most effective sequencing and timing of the pairing of these stimuli. They are contiguity behaviourists.

Skinner, on the other hand, was less concerned with the part played by the initial stimulus in bringing about learning, attaching a far greater importance to the consequence which follows a response. He is thus a reinforcement behaviourist. Skinner called any consequence which increases the frequency of a response occurring, a reinforcer. The food which is dispensed by the Skinner box when the rat presses the lever is thus a reinforcer as it increases the likelihood of the rat pressing the lever again. Skinner suggested that if a response is reinforced, it is strengthened and is therefore more likely to occur again. Reinforcement is thus a key factor in bringing about learning. A total lack of reinforcement would lead to the connection between stimulus and response disappearing altogether.

Reinforcement also serves an additional purpose in that it indicates whether the response given is the desired response. It confirms that the response is the correct response to that particular stimulus. Reinforcement is thus a form of external feedback. We all need feedback when in a learning situation – ballet dancers practise in front of a mirror for this very reason.

Suppose, however, that instead of learning ballet, you are learning to wire an electrical plug. How do you know you are doing it correctly? You are fairly certain that you are following the instructions correctly and it looks to be similar to the example you were shown, but is it actually correct? You need confirmation or knowledge of results. Without this you may be practising wiring your plug in an incorrect manner and if this becomes habitual, it will be more difficult for you to learn the correct procedure. We react to or act upon the external environment. We cannot provide our own feedback and so it needs to be come from an external source. Thus when teaching, you need to constantly supply your learners with feedback on their performance.

Immediate knowledge of results is required to supply feedback to the learner.

Skinner was not the first to study reinforcement and in fact built on the earlier work of Thorndike.

Thorndike, cats and pleasurable consequences

Thorndike's most famous experiment centred on how cats learned to escape from puzzle boxes. A cat was placed inside a cage with a latch on the door and a piece of salmon outside of the cage, visible but just out of the cat's reach. Typically, after failing to reach the salmon, the cat tried to get out of the cage in a purely random fashion, scratching at the bars and moving around inside the cage. Eventually, purely by chance, the cat hit the latch on the door and the door opened, allowing access to the salmon. With the repetition of this experiment, the amount of time spent in escaping became less and the door of the cage was opened sooner.

Thorndike called this type of learning 'trial and error' learning as there was a gradual decrease in errors leading to a quicker escape time. What is of particular interest when considering reinforcement, however, is Thorndike's interest in the nature of the consequences of the response. He made a distinction between pleasurable and unpleasant consequences, which is expressed in his law of effect. This law states that responses which are followed by pleasurable consequences are more likely to be repeated or as Thorndike expresses it, 'stamped in'. The opposite, although considered less important by Thorndike, also applies – responses which lead to unpleasurable consequences are less likely to be repeated, or 'stamped out'.

Skinner preferred the neutral concept of 'reinforcement', as pleasurable and unpleasurable consequences suggested an element of subjectivity in their definition. Regardless of whether we agree with Skinner or accept Thorndike's position, what can be stated with certainty is that reinforcement plays a crucial part in establishing stimulus–response connections.

Let us return to Pavlov's dog for a moment and consider a situation whereby Pavlov repeatedly rings his bell and, on cue, the dog salivates. Pavlov doesn't, however, give the dog any food at the same time on any of these occasions. If this were the case, the dog would eventually stop salivating to the sound of the bell. In other words, the conditioned response would gradually become weaker and finally disappear. This is known as extinction.

> *Extinction occurs when a response decreases in frequency because it no longer leads to reinforcement.*
>
> (Ormrod, 2008, p67)

Ormrod illustrates this by referring to learners who are never called on when they raise their hands and subsequently stop trying to participate in class discussions. Perhaps the most famous example of extinction, however, is the case of the boy who cried wolf. The story tells us that the boy was left on the hillside to look after the sheep in the evening while the shepherd went to the warm tavern at the bottom of the hill to relax after a hard day's work, with the promise that he would come to the boy's assistance if the local wolf came visiting. This arrangement seemed to work well for a few nights but eventually the boy became bored and so to liven up his evening he cried *Wolf!*, extracting much merriment from the sight of the shepherd rushing up the hill to his assistance. Needless to say the shepherd was not very pleased and muttering to himself, he retreated back down the hill to the warmth of the tavern. This scene was repeated several times over the coming weeks. One night, however, the wolf decided to put in an appearance. The boy immediately shouted *Wolf!* at the top of his voice but no help was forthcoming from the shepherd. As there had been a lack of reinforcement on previous occasions of shouting for help (no wolf appeared), the stimulus (the cry of *Wolf!*) no longer brought about the desired response (the shepherd coming to the boy's assistance) and the wolf was able to dine uninterrupted on a main course of now-silent boy after polishing off a small lamb starter.

While it would not be necessary for Pavlov to produce food every time he rang the bell, he would have to pair the food (unconditioned stimulus) with the bell (conditioned stimulus) on some occasions if he wished to maintain the behaviour pattern he had established. Even an occasional appearance of the wolf would have been enough to save the boy. Similarly, Skinner's rat would not have to gain access to food every time it pressed the lever in response to the light. It would have to receive food on some occasions, however, to maintain its lever-pressing behaviour.

It was Skinner's belief that even low levels of reinforcement would give rise to effective learning and maintain that learning over a period of time before extinction took place. He later devised a series of different reinforcement schedules in an attempt to establish the relationship between the maintenance of behaviour and the frequency of reinforcement.

Reinforcement can take different forms and it is important to identify these before we consider the management of behaviour in Chapter 3.

PRACTICAL TASK PRACTICAL TASK **PRACTICAL TASK** PRACTICAL TASK **PRACTICAL TASK**

A grumpy old man works night shifts and so sleeps during the day. When the local children come home from school they deliberately stand outside the man's bedroom window making a noise. The man jumps out of bed, rushes outside and shouts at the children. They run off down the street, laughing, and the grumpy old man goes back to bed to catch up on his sleep. One day, the grumpy old man buys some earplugs. He doesn't hear the children any more and soon they stop making a noise outside his bedroom window. Why is this?

Check your answers with those at the end of the chapter before reading on.

Reinforcement and punishment

So far, we have focused on instances where reinforcement has been achieved by rewarding the appropriate behaviour. A learner answers a question correctly, the teacher responds with a smile and a word of praise. This type of reinforcement is known as positive reinforcement; reinforcement because it increases the likelihood of the required response, positive because it 'adds' to the situation.

Suppose, however, that a learner does not do their homework and is repeatedly told off by the teacher. On the following occasion on which homework is due, the learner produces the homework to avoid being told off again. This is still a form of reinforcement as it has increased the likelihood of the desired behaviour (completing the homework), but this time instead of 'adding' to the situation, something has been removed. The homework has been completed not to gain praise (although the teacher will undoubtedly use praise when receiving the homework to further reinforce this behaviour), but to remove the possibility of being told off. This type of reinforcement is known as negative reinforcement. In the same way that we associate positive reinforcement with reward, we can consider negative reinforcement to be concerned with relief.

Negative reinforcement is often confused with punishment but there is a critical difference between the two. While reinforcement is designed to strengthen or increase the likelihood of a given behaviour, punishment is intended to weaken or eliminate a given behaviour. In the same way that there are two different types of reinforcement, there are also two types of punishment.

A learner who misbehaves is given a detention – at the end of the class, when everyone else leaves, they have to stay behind and complete a task. This is a punishment as its purpose is to prevent the occurrence of this type of behaviour in the future. Another learner who misbehaves is told that as a result of their misbehaviour they will not be allowed to go on a trip that has been organised for the following week. This also is a punishment as similarly, the desired outcome is the prevention of this type of behaviour in the future. There is a significant difference between the two forms of punishment, however. The first is known as presentation punishment as it presents an unpleasant consequence, while the second is called removal punishment as it leads to the removal of some form of privilege or right.

PRACTICAL TASK PRACTICAL TASK **PRACTICAL TASK** PRACTICAL TASK **PRACTICAL TASK**

Make sure you are clear about the differences between reinforcement and punishment by completing this short exercise. Look at the examples below and decide if they demonstrate positive reinforcement (PR), negative reinforcement (NR), presentation punishment (PP) or removal punishment (RP). The first one is done for you. Check your answers against the table at the end of the chapter before reading on.

The teacher praises a correct response	PR
The corporal is reduced to the ranks for drinking on duty	
The motorist receives a £60 fine for parking on double yellow lines	
The driver of a car puts on their seat belt to stop that annoying buzzer	
The teenager is banned from watching television for being rude to their mother	
The insurance salesperson gets a bonus for achieving their monthly target	
The boxer receives a public warning for hitting below the belt	
The teenager tidies their bedroom to stop their parents' nagging	
The footballer receives congratulations from his team mates upon scoring a goal	

Behaviourism and motivation

The concept of reinforcement summarises the behaviourist approach to motivation – what makes us do what we do. Motivation, in common with other major features of behaviourism is external to the person. It is the desire to pursue a goal in order to receive external reinforcement which normally takes the form of a reward of some kind.

> *Motivation in the behaviourist world is extrinsic in nature. Learning is encouraged by a reward of some description.*

REFLECTIVE TASK

List the extrinsic motivators that influence you in your daily life.

Now list the extrinsic motivators that can be used in teaching.

Can you identify any potential dangers in relying solely on extrinsic motivation?

Extrinsic motivators abound in everyday life. In terms of career, for instance, a pay rise, qualifications, promotion and increased status can all be extrinsic motivators. The desire to be accepted, admired or approved of by others are typical social motivators. In teaching and learning, it is widely accepted that intrinsic factors such as curiosity or successfully rising to a challenge represent the more effective form of motivation, particularly when considering the quality and longevity of learning that can be attained. The very fact that intrinsic motivation is internal to the learner means, however, that teachers cannot directly affect or 'tap into' it. The teacher's management of motivation is by necessity reliant on extrinsic motivators.

The list of extrinsic motivators is fairly long and to some extent learners are conditioned into an expectation of extrinsic motivation from an early age through strategies such displays of work on classroom walls, gold stars, house points and commendation letters, which are used fairly extensively in the school setting. The strategies used in the lifelong learning sector are slightly more subtle in character and include:

- positive comments on written work;
- praise;
- teacher enthusiasm;
- positive body language;
- active listening by the teacher;
- explaining the benefits of what is to be learned at the beginning of a teaching session;
- nominating learners to answer questions only if we are confident they can do so;
- showing an interest in learners as individuals.

Quite often learners need an initial 'nudge' to arouse their interest and this is the intention behind the use of extrinsic motivators – to initially engage learners hoping that intrinsic motivation will take over and become the main driving force behind the learning that is to take place. Extrinsic means are used to create a climate in which intrinsic motivation will grow and prosper.

There are, however, a number of problems that can arise in using extrinsic motivation. These stem from the fact that whatever we are extrinsically motivated to do, we do to gain a reward rather than for the enjoyment of learning.

Perhaps one of the extrinsic motivators you identified was a test or exam. This can lead to cramming or learning the required material for the sole purpose of passing the test or exam. Once the test or exam has been successfully negotiated, the learned material is forgotten as it has served its purpose. Generally, behaviour changes brought about through extrinsic motivation can be temporary, lasting only as long as it takes to gain the resultant reward. Learning is seen as a means to an end. This point of view underpins a somewhat cynical but fairly popular view of the Educational Maintenance Allowance (EMA). The motivation to attend classes is to get that all-important signature on the EMA form and the resultant money, rather than to necessarily engage in learning.

A further danger lies in the possibility that extrinsic motivators may be overused. If praise, for instance, is used indiscriminately, it becomes a normal expectation and so loses its effect as a reinforcement strategy. If a reward is given as a matter of course, the level of reward has to increase so as to maintain the same level of performance and eventually a situation may be reached where learning will be engaged in only if a reward is on offer. Used appropriately and sparingly, however, extrinsic motivators can be an effective tool and can be used to nurture a more intrinsic approach to learning.

Generalisation and the transfer of learning

Transfer of learning can be defined as *learning in one situation affects learning in another situation*. If you are proficient at roller-skating and then decide to go ice-skating for the first time, you would probably find it an easier skill to acquire than someone who had never previously roller-skated. Your roller-skating skills would transfer to the ice-skating environment and so your previous learning about roller-skating would assist you in your new learning about ice-skating. Transfer would be said to have taken place. Because this particular type of transfer is helpful, it is termed positive transfer.

The opposite situation would occur, however, if, having learned to water ski, you now learned to ski on snow. The habit of leaning backwards required for water skiing would definitely not help you to stay upright when skiing on snow. Hence this type of transfer is termed negative transfer. It will by now be apparent that in order for either type of transfer to take place there must be similarities between the two situations. According to Thorndike's 'identical elements theory of transfer', it is the degree of similarity between the two situations that determines the amount of transfer that takes place.

Transfer is an important goal in teaching and learning. If you teach French to students in a classroom, you want them to be able to make themselves understood if they go to France. You are looking to them to transfer their classroom skills to the real world. Similarly, you would hope that skills learned in the motor vehicle workshop in college would be transferred to working life in a garage. So, how likely is transfer if a behaviourist approach to teaching and learning is adopted? What degree of similarity is required between two different situations?

Consider Pavlov's dog. It has learned to salivate to a bell which makes a sound of a particular pitch. If a bell is now rung which is of a slightly higher or lower pitch, it will still salivate. This is known as stimulus generalisation – the dog is responding in the same manner to a stimulus which is similar to the original one. If, however, bells of increasingly different pitch to the original bell are used, the amount of salivation will soon decrease and eventually stop altogether. The dog is now said to be exhibiting stimulus discrimination.

The possibility of transfer of learning can be increased if possibilities are pointed out and practice is given in as large a variety of situations as possible. Generally, however, the range of generalisation is fairly narrow when a behavioural approach is adopted and so transfer occurs only when there is a large degree of similarity between situations.

Transfer of learning is limited in a behaviourist approach to teaching and learning.

A SUMMARY OF **KEY POINTS**

> The need for a scientific approach in psychology, based on objectivity and measurability gave rise to the behaviourist perspective.

> Behaviourism focuses on and interprets the world in terms of externally observable behaviour.

> The more prominent behaviourists are Watson, Pavlov (classical conditioning), Thorndike and Skinner (operant conditioning).

> Pavlov introduced classical conditioning, whereby an existing involuntary reflex action can be paired with a different stimulus to that which would naturally initiate it.

> Learning is considered to consist of a change in behaviour brought about by some form of action or experience.

> The change in behaviour comes about as a result of the establishment of a simple stimulus–response pattern. Each reaction is an exact response to a specific stimulus.

> In operant conditioning, Skinner emphasises the role of reinforcement in increasing the likelihood of a given stimulus evoking the appropriate response.

> Operant conditioning brings about new and original behaviours and learning can be built up into more complex forms by a step-by-step process. The teacher shapes the behaviour of the learner towards predetermined objectives.

> Motivation is controlled extrinsically by reinforcement or punishment.

> Transfer is limited and only occurs when two situations are very similar.

> Immediate knowledge of results is important. The required response is reinforced by successful performance, especially if this is rewarded.

Answers to practical tasks

The story of Jenny and Johnny

(a) The sight of Jenny is the initial unconditioned stimulus as it causes the reflex action of the 'warm feeling inside'.

(b) The 'warm feeling inside' becomes the conditioned response when it occurs as a result of the song being played.

(c) The song is initially the neutral stimulus as Johnny is unaffected by it. It becomes the conditioned stimulus when it is associated with the 'warm feeling inside' and causes this response to occur in Johnny.

(d) When the 'warm feeling inside' occurs as a result of seeing Jenny, it is the unconditioned response as it is a natural reflex action at this stage.

The grumpy old man

The stimulus (bedroom window) initiates a response of making a noise. The children enjoy the sight of the grumpy old man shouting at them in his pyjamas. His appearance thus reinforces their behaviour. When he stops shouting at them there is a lack of reinforcement and so extinction occurs. The stimulus no longer causes the same response.

Reinforcement and Punishment

The teacher praises a correct response	PR
The corporal is reduced to the ranks for drinking on duty	RP
The motorist receives a £60 fine for parking on double yellow lines	PP
The driver of a car puts on his seat belt to stop that annoying buzzer	NR
The teenage boy is banned from watching television for being rude to his mother	RP
The insurance salesman gets a bonus for achieving his monthly target	PR
The boxer receives a public warning for hitting below the belt	PP
The teenage girl tidies her bedroom to stop her parents' nagging	NR
The footballer receives congratulations from his team mates upon scoring a goal	PR

REFERENCES REFERENCES **REFERENCES** REFERENCES **REFERENCES** REFERENCES

Hergenhahn, BR and Olson, MH (2001) *An introduction to theories of learning.* Harlow: Pearson Education.

Lefrançois, GR (1999) *Psychology for teaching* (10th edn). Belmont: Wadsworth.

Ormrod, J (2008) *Human learning* (5th edn). New Jersey: Pearson Prentice Hall.

Pavlov, IP (1927) *Conditioned reflexes: an investigation of the physiological activity of the verebral cortex.* London: Oxford University Press.

Skinner, BF (1953) *Science and human behaviour.* New York: The Free Press.

Sousa, DA (2006) *How the brain learns.* London: Sage.

Watson, JB (1919) *Psychology from the standpoint of a behaviorist.* Philadelphia: Lippincott.

3
Implications of behaviourism for practice

Chapter overview and objectives

The way in which we teach depends upon our view of learning and how it takes place. In this chapter we consider the behaviourist view of learning and the type of classroom practice that is consistent with that particular perspective. The general areas covered are planning, teaching methods, assessment and classroom management.

When you have worked through this chapter you will be able to:

- **recognise the fundamental role of objectives in the planning process;**
- **state the characteristics of a well-written objective;**
- **recognise the contribution of behaviourism to curriculum design and planning;**
- **describe the relationship between behaviourism, programmed learning and E-learning;**
- **explain why 'closed questioning' is associated with a behaviourist approach;**
- **carry out a skills analysis;**
- **identify a range of items used in objective testing;**
- **explain how objective- and criterion-based skills assessment contribute to the reliability and validity of the results obtained.**

This chapter contributes to the following values and areas of professional knowledge as contained in the LLUK professional standards for teachers, tutors and trainers in the lifelong learning sector:

AS4, BS2, CS4, DS3

AK1.1, AK4.1, AK4.3, BK1.1, BK1.2, BK1.3, BK2.1, BK2.7, CK3.1

Introduction

In the previous chapter, you learned about behaviourist views on learning. The style and manner of anyone's teaching are inevitably based upon their view of learning. This chapter will examine the implications of a behaviourist perspective on learning for the way in which teaching is organised and conducted. Essentially, the approach adopted will use methods of delivery most appropriate to bringing about a 'change in behaviour' and rely on assessment methods that will most effectively check whether or not the desired change in behaviour has in fact taken place. Later in this chapter, we will explore these different aspects of teaching but we will start off by looking at planning. Teachers plan in lots of different ways. Some will start with a consideration of the resources at their disposal; others will start from the content they want to include in the lesson. Some will think first about the types of activities that will work well, others still will consider the potential challenges presented by the particular group they will teach, or even the time of day that they will teach them, and plan their lessons in the light of these factors. None of these, however, would constitute a starting point in planning for a behaviourist.

Planning from a behaviourist perspective

For a behaviourist the planning of a teaching session would start from an initial statement of the change in behaviour, or the learning, that is to be brought about. This change in behaviour can take the form of the attainment of new knowledge, the acquisition of a new skill or a change in attitude. These three different types of change are often referred to as the cognitive domain (knowledge), the psycho-motor domain (skills) and the affective domain (attitudes) of learning, although they are commonly and more simply referred to as knowledge, skills and attitude domains.

REFLECTIVE TASK

Here are two statements of learning that might apply to a teaching session.

1. Develop an understanding of silver service place settings.
2. State the utensils that would be present in a place setting for a four-course silver service meal.

Of these two statements, which do you think a behaviourist would be more likely to use? Why might they be less enthusiastic about the other?

Having read the previous chapter, which stresses an observable change in behaviour, you will undoubtedly have identified the flaw that a behaviourist would pick out in statement 1. *Develop an understanding of...* describes a process that occurs in the mind and so does not fit with a behavioural view of learning. *State the utensils that...* would be much more acceptable to a behaviourist as it specifies a behaviour – 'state' – that can be observed (or perhaps in this case, heard) and easily measured. The secret in arriving at a statement which is easily measurable lies in choosing an appropriate verb such as 'state' which describes an observable behaviour. Such verbs are commonly known as action verbs, to stress the fact that they need to identify an outcome that can be evidenced by some form of action on the part of the learner rather than through an internal mental process such as 'understand'. Statement 2 then, identifies the learning or change in behaviour that is to take place in a manner that is acceptable to a behaviourist.

Such a statement is commonly referred to as a learning objective and would normally be prefaced with a phrase like:

by the end of this session, each learner will be able to...

As they are derived from a behaviourist perspective, well-written learning objectives are considered to possess the characteristics spelled out in the mnemonic, SMART. Francis and Gould (2009, p62) interpret this as in the following manner.

Specific – the objective should describe the desired learning exactly, stating clearly what the learner will be able to do as a result of participating in the teaching session. This is achieved by use of an appropriate action verb. The action verb is the word which comes immediately after *will be able to...*

Measurable – what the learner will be able to do should be observable. It should result in some form of action that satisfies the teacher that learning has indeed taken place. This may be through listing, naming, explaining, recognising, demonstrating, performing or any other action through which learners can demonstrate they *are able to . . .*

Achievable – clarity is all very well but to be of any practical use, the stated learning must be within the capabilities of the intended learners. After all, it is they who *will be able to . . .*

Relevant – what is the point of this learning that the objective describes? If learners cannot see why it is important or how it will help them, they may ask themselves why they should bother *to be able to . . .*

Time-bound – What is the timescale within which this learning is to take place? It may be one teaching session, a week or even a lifetime of trying, but learners should be made aware of how long they have to *be able to . . .*

In writing knowledge or skill objectives, it should be possible to arrive at a SMART statement without too much difficulty. If the temptation to use 'know' or 'understand' is still strong and you cannot readily find an alternative phrasing, ask yourself how you would assess for the knowledge or understanding you seek. This will often suggest an appropriate action verb. Attitude objectives on the other hand, are by their very nature, much more difficult to pin down.

In his seminal book *Preparing instructional objectives*, Robert F Mager (1975, p21) suggests that a well-written objective should include the following characteristics.

1. **Performance**. An objective always says what a learner is expected to be able to *do*.
2. **Conditions**. An objective always describes the important conditions (if any) under which the performance is to occur.
3. **Criterion**. Whenever possible, an objective describes the criterion of acceptable performance by describing how well the learner must perform in order to be considered acceptable.

He suggests the following as a good example:

> *Given a linear algebraic equation with one unknown, be able to solve (write the solution) for the unknown without the aid of references, tables or calculating devices.*
>
> (Mager, 1975, p50)

While it is not necessary to go to quite those lengths while writing learning objectives for a teaching session, it should now be evident why there is often an insistence that verbs like 'know', 'think' and 'appreciate' are inappropriate when writing a SMART learning objective or outcome. These refer to mental processes and as such do not conform to a behaviourist view of learning. To make sure an objective is both specific and measurable, processes such as 'know' and 'understand' are replaced by words like *list*, *identify*, *define*, *state* and *explain*. These are known as action verbs. The required *action* verb does exactly what it says – it describes an action or observable behaviour. Without this it would be very difficult to assess whether or not the specified learning or change in behaviour had taken place.

PRACTICAL TASK PRACTICAL TASK **PRACTICAL TASK** PRACTICAL TASK **PRACTICAL TASK**

From the list below, tick the words you might use to write SMART objectives. Check your answers against those at the end of the chapter before reading on.

define		choose		describe		differentiate between	
state		appreciate		calculate		identify	
report		list		understand		know	
comprehend		perform		sympathise with		explain	
recognise		be aware of		classify		draw	
select		sort		demonstrate		be conscious of	

According to a behaviourist perspective, planning should start from a clear statement of the final expected outcome, phrased in terms of the expected behaviour change. One of the perceived advantages of this approach is that it leads to a systematic approach to planning. Once the learning that is to take place has been identified and stated in an appropriate manner, other planning decisions can be made concerning:

- the content of the session which is required to achieve this;
- the most appropriate methods and activities to deliver this content;
- the resources required to support the chosen methods and activities;
- the assessment techniques which will best determine whether or not the identified learning has taken place;
- how best to evaluate the session.

Because it provides a structured, procedural approach to planning, this approach is nearly always introduced into initial teacher training programmes; it provides a logical, step-by-step method of planning and organising teaching sessions.

This systematic approach to planning forms the basis of the 'Product' model of curriculum, so called because it emphasises the products or outcomes in the learning process. This model was championed by Ralph Tyler (1949) in his book *Basic principles of curriculum and instruction* and at the time was considered to have brought a new degree of clarity to the planning process.

The model below, known as the 'Rational curriculum model' or more popularly nowadays as the 'Training cycle' is derived from Tyler's work and sets out the systematic approach to planning.

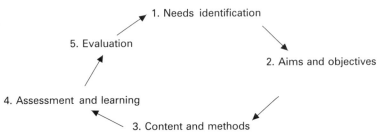

1. Needs identification
2. Aims and objectives
3. Content and methods
4. Assessment and learning
5. Evaluation

There has been a move away from the term 'learning objective' and a move towards the term 'learning outcome' and indeed many writers use the terms interchangeably. There was great debate in the 1970s about the use of objectives and their emphasis on observable behaviour. Learning could take other forms, it was argued, and the narrow, objectives-based approach was unsuitable in such instances. This is a debate which will be continued in Chapter 5 when approaches to planning from a cognitive perspective are considered. One result of this debate, however, was a move towards curriculum planning based around outcomes (Prideaux, 2000, p168). There seems to be some agreement that outcomes are related to competence (Marsh, 2004, p28; Hillier, 2005, p90; Gray, Griffin and Nasta, 2000, p89) and are often related to vocational subjects but they are by no means limited to this area of curriculum. Marsh (2004, p28) suggests that:

> Outcome statements concentrate upon the outputs rather than the inputs of teaching. Exponents of this approach argue that objectives only concentrate upon the inputs of teaching.

While outcomes do appear to be written in less behavioural terms than objectives, whatever the distinction between the two, they share a common purpose in that they try to express what is required of the learner in an unambiguous and measurable fashion. Perhaps it is this common purpose rather than academic distinctions which matter most to us as teachers.

You will notice in the above model that the planning process actually starts not from an objective or outcome, but with the expression of an aim or aims. Aims are much more general than either objectives or outcomes, and set out to state the purpose or intention of the teacher or teaching session as a whole. They differ therefore from both objectives and outcomes which express what is required of the learner. The aim in writing this chapter, for instance, is *to introduce the various practical implications of a behaviourist perspective on learning*. An objective or outcome that might be expected of you upon reading the chapter, might be to *state the characteristics of a well-written objective.*

Despite the popularity of the above model, teaching unfortunately does not fit very easily into a 'one size fits all' mould as the objectives debate of the 1970s suggests and it may well be that you find difficulty in fitting your planning around this approach. If this is the case, you may well be working from a different definition of learning than that favoured by behaviourists. It will be seen in later chapters that different perspectives on learning necessitate different approaches to planning and indeed all other aspects of the process of teaching.

Returning to behaviourism, however, having looked at what is to be learned, attention is now focused on how this is to be achieved.

Teaching methods

Behaviourist approaches to teaching and learning are often associated with drills and repetition and in its most extreme form, behaviourism can adopt this rote approach to learning. Perhaps you remember learning your times table in exactly such a fashion? There is much more to behaviourism, however, than rote learning.

From programmed learning to e-learning

A direct application of the work of Skinner can be found in programmed learning – the forerunner of its modern counterpart, computer-assisted learning. The principle behind programmed learning is the presentation of small chunks of information to the learner who then has to make a response which is checked before moving on to the next chunk of information in the series. Each of these presentations is known as a frame. In the early stages of programmed learning, frames were brought into view through a small window on the top of a wooden box by turning a handle on the side of the box. The result was similar to that shown below.

This is a typical frame. It contains some information, a question and an answer What does the frame contain? That's right – some information, a question and an answer	← The learner turns the handle to view the first chuck of information ← A second turn of the handle allows the learner to respond to the question ← The response is reinforced by the next turn of the handle

The learner reads the information and is then required to actively respond to the question What is required of the learner? An active response to the question	← The handle is turned again to reveal the top of the next frame ← A second turn of the handle allows the learner to respond to the question ← The response is reinforced by the next turn of the handle

The answer provides reinforcement through knowledge of results How does the answer provide reinforcement? Through knowledge of results	← And so on until the series of smaller chunks of information is built up into a more complex segment of knowledge

A series of frames such as those above would constitute a linear programme as the frames would be encountered and worked through in a sequential manner. It is possible, however, to construct a branching programme which allows learners to take an individual path depending on their existing knowledge. This is achieved by allowing the learner to select from a number of answers to the question that is asked. The choice of answer determines the next point on the programme to which the learner is directed. This strategy has been adapted to textbooks where at the end of a page of information, the reader is asked to answer a question and is then directed to another page of information depending upon the answer given.

These days, a more sophisticated approach is taken through computer-aided learning, one strand of the movement towards electronic or e-learning which is currently being encouraged in the lifelong learning sector. Computers have the capacity to add sound to the presentation and employ superior graphics and in some cases, animations. There is thus a greater opportunity to present more information at one time and links to other supplementary sources on the world wide web can be easily created. More complex and active responses can also be required from the user. Despite this more visually attractive and versatile method of presentation, computer-assisted learning is still underpinned by the same Skinnerian principles as its more humble predecessor – the wooden box.

REFLECTIVE TASK

Among teachers, opinions are divided concerning the effectiveness and desirability of computer-assisted learning. What do you consider to be the compelling arguments either for or against this approach? On balance are you in favour of computer-assisted learning or do you have reservations?

Some of the perceived advantages of computer-assisted learning are:

- learning from a computer can be seen as an attractive approach, leading to greater receptivity;
- learners work at their own pace, thus allowing for some differentiation;
- it affords the teacher an opportunity for individual contact;
- immediate knowledge of results is given;
- the embarrassment of giving wrong answers in public is removed.

Once the novelty of the method has worn off, however, motivation can be adversely affected, and the fact that learners work at their own pace does not necessarily mean that they are working to their full capacity. The major objections to computer-assisted learning are:

- the lack of social interaction and the loss of the learning that can arise from this;
- the method is only as effective as the programme that it uses and it could be argued that m*ost of it is presently just e-information, not yet e-learning* (Race, 2005, p177).

Whatever view is held, computer-assisted learning, with its roots in behaviourist learning theory, does provide another strategy to be used in meeting the different needs of learners, increasing the likelihood of an inclusive approach to teaching.

The use of questioning

Teachers ask questions for a variety of reasons: to see what learners already know, to check if learning has taken place, to make learners think, to challenge assumptions, to encourage participation, to ensure attention, to introduce a topic, to arouse curiosity.

REFLECTIVE TASK

Which of the following questions on page 29 do you think are more likely to be asked in a 'behaviourist' approach to learning?

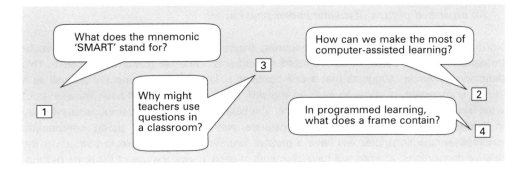

Generally, a behaviourist approach favours closed questions as this type of question assumes there is a 'right' answer. Questions 1 and 4 fall into this category. Each is being used to check if learning has taken place. Has the desired change in behaviour taken place? Has the correct response been given to the stimulus question? Questions such as these are explored further in the section on assessment.

Closed questions can also be used in a learning rather than an assessment context. The previous section on programmed and computer-assisted learning has shown how it is possible to build up a fairly complex piece of knowledge by adopting a step-by-step approach. A similar approach can sometimes be taken using closed questions although it may involve some previous knowledge on the part of the learner. Rather than present smaller chunks of information, these can be arrived at by the use of closed questioning, thus making for a more active learning session and creating opportunities for reinforcement.

The method adopted is to write down the different bits of information that are to be acquired in a list in the correct sequence. The list is scanned to see what will need to be told to learners and what can be arrived at through questioning. Having identified suitable areas, closed questions can be devised which will lead to the desired responses. By making the required answer the starting point the questions arrived at should be sufficiently closed to lead learners to the 'correct' response.

REFLECTIVE TASK

Identify a subject you currently teach by 'telling'. Devise a series of closed questions that could be used to impart the same information. Use a grid similar to that shown below to structure this task, expanding it as necessary

Information	Question to draw out information
1.	
2.	
3.	

The teaching of skills

Before turning to the methods used in the teaching of practical skills it is worth first of all, exploring the nature of a skill itself. One way of achieving this is by starting from the definition. One definition of skill is:

An organised pattern of mental and/or physical activity.

Normally a practical skill such as wallpapering, plastering or bricklaying for example, would be considered as a series of co-ordinated movements – after all this is what is seen. This definition, however, suggests that a skill contains a 'knowledge' component as well as a 'doing' component. In order to perform the skill, the learner must first have knowledge of what has to be done and in what sequence. The balance of these two components will vary in different skills. Riding a bicycle, for instance, will have a greater 'doing' component, whereas using a computer will have a greater 'knowledge' component, but whatever the relative proportions, all skills will have elements of each, hence the use of the term 'psycho-motor' for this domain of learning.

Generally, demonstration is used to impart the 'knowledge' component of a skill and this is followed up with practice accompanied by feedback so learners can acquire the 'doing' component. A typical skills session will contain both of these activities, the nature of the skill determining the relative amounts of each.

This practice fits a behaviourist view of skills acquisition as proposed by Fitts and Posner (1968), which suggests the process occurs in three stages.

1. The cognitive phase – the learner identifies what has to be done and how to do it.
2. The associative phase – the learner develops the appropriate S–R connections by practising the skill. Reinforcement is achieved through external feedback.
3. The autonomous phase – performance of the skill becomes automatic.

The nature of a skill can also be examined by looking at the characteristics of skilled performance. What is it that sets apart those who are skilled from those who are not? If you were to observe two different people hanging wallpaper, one a novice and the other an old hand, how would you be able to tell which was which? Some of the telltale signs would be evident in the way that each went about the task, others in the result obtained.

REFLECTIVE TASK

Using the example of wallpapering, list below the signs of skilled and non-skilled practice you would expect to see:
(a) in the performance of the skill;
(b) in the end product achieved.

The novice wallpaper hanger would undoubtedly be less confident in their approach, may well have had to re-hang some rolls either because they were cut wrongly, the wallpaper paste dried too quickly or they used their brush in an awkward manner and would definitely have taken a longer time than the old hand to complete the job. The finished job would probably not line up as well, contain air bubbles and may well have used more paper to cover the same area of wall.

In general terms, the kind of characteristics of skilled performance one might expect to see include the following.

- Economy of movement – all unnecessary movements will have been eliminated from the performance of the skill. Movement in general will be kept to a minimum, cutting down on the effort required.
- Ease, smoothness – movements will flow without any awkwardness or jerking.
- Continuity, confidence – different parts of the skill will join seamlessly and be carried out in a confident manner and without hesitation.
- Lack of fatigue – as a result of the characteristics above, fatigue will be kept to a minimum and the skill can be carried out for a prolonged period of time.

The end product would be:

- of a high quality;
- completed in a reasonable time;
- achieved with a minimum of wastage of materials.

Perhaps the biggest difference in the two performances, however, would be the extent to which it had become 'automatic' as far as the old hand was concerned.

Those who are involved in the training of skills are normally themselves skilled performers and will exhibit the above characteristics. By the time we have become skilled, most of what we do has become automatic; we do not have to think about it. Because of this we may not even be aware of all of the actions that we make and consequently often make too many assumptions concerning what learners already know.

This can be remedied by conducting a skills analysis prior to demonstration. The main purpose of a skills analysis is to highlight:

- all of the specific actions involved in the skill;
- the exact sequence of these actions;
- the sensory information required at each stage;
- any decisions that have to be made in the execution of the skill;
- any particular difficulties associated with the skill.

This is achieved by breaking down the overall skill into a number of sub-skills. Each sub-skill is then broken down further until a level of detail appropriate to the prospective learners is reached as shown below.

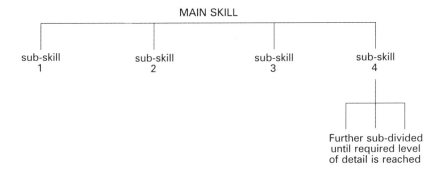

Consider the example below.

This shows the first level of analysis which will then be further broken down until an appropriate level of detail is achieved.

Skills analysis also helps learners when it comes to the practice element. The total skill has been simplified by breaking it down into these smaller sub-skills, which are not unlike Skinner's successive approximations (see previous chapter). This allows the skill to be learned in a sequence of more manageable sequential units, each one being mastered in turn, thus building up to the more complex main skill in a step-by step-manner. The mastering of each sub-skill also has important consequences for motivation.

In terms of practice then, we can note some important points.

Demonstration
The demonstration provides the knowledge required to perform the skill. As already pointed out, a skills analysis should be conducted to ensure that this knowledge is most effectively communicated in a comprehensive and systematic manner. Sometimes a skill is best observed from the position of the user and so positioning of learners during the demonstration has to be taken into consideration. It goes without saying that wherever you decide the most appropriate position to be, all learners must be able to see and hear clearly. Demonstration often starts with an example of the complete process to help establish the cognitive phase of skills acquisition (refer back to Fitts and Posner), before breaking it down into the component parts identified by skills analysis. The accompanying commentary at this stage will be informed by the results of the final stage of the skills analysis. The different sub-skills are then linked together in a final demonstration of the complete skill.

Practice
Learners are now ready to move on to the associative phase of skill acquisition and this is achieved through practice, which should take place as soon as possible after the demonstration. Practice involves the mastering the various sub-skills, each of these sub-skills building upon the previous one until the complete skill is acquired. How do learners know that their practice is correct? As we have seen, behaviourism discounts processes internal to the learner, focusing on the interaction with the external environment. The role of the teacher during practice sessions then, is to provide both reinforcement and feedback by supplying knowledge of results. Correct practice is acknowledged and praise is given where appropriate. Guidance is given where necessary to prevent the practice of incorrect responses and to generally improve performance. External feedback and guidance are essential components of the practice phase.

Assessment of learning

When learning objectives which are concerned with knowledge are assessed, answers are sought that demonstrate the specific change in behaviour that the teaching has intended to bring about. The learner is required to give the appropriate response to a given stimulus.

Thus, the stimulus of *six times three* should encourage a response of 18. If the response was 19 or 17 it would be considered to be incorrect in each case. Assessment of knowledge-related learning objectives then, is a matter of using strategies that will seek out the one correct answer (response) to the question or problem (stimulus). An objective test is designed to fulfil this function as it is defined as *a series of items each of which has a predetermined correct answer* (Walklin, 1982, p315).

An objective test can consist of a variety of different types of questions or items whose common characteristic is that they have only that one predetermined correct answer as stated above. Try the short test on behaviourism below and note the different types of questions or items that it contains.

PRACTICAL TASK PRACTICAL TASK **PRACTICAL TASK** PRACTICAL TASK **PRACTICAL TASK**

Complete the test below – check your answers at the end of the chapter before reading on.

Objective test on behaviourism

Q1. What is the name of the type of conditioning associated with Skinner?

. . . .

Q2. Fill in the gaps in the following sentence.

In behaviourism learning occurs through the association of a. . . . . with a

specific. . . . . and anything that strengthens that connection between the two is

known as a . . . .
Q3. Is the following statement true or false?

Punishment increases the likelihood of the desired behaviour.

Put a cross through the wrong answer:

                        TRUE   FALSE

Q4. Pick out the correct answer to the question from the options listed below.

Question: Which of the following 'action' verbs would you use when writing a learning objective?

(a) think
(b) understand
(c) state
(d) know

Answer. . . . .

Q5. Place the following stages of the training cycle in the correct order.

(a) Content and methods
(b) Evaluation
(c) Needs identification
(d) Assessment of learning
(e) Aims and objectives

Answer
  1.
  2.
  3.
  4.
  5.

Q6. Correctly match the items in the two following lists.

List A
1.   Question 1 in this test
2.   Question 2 in this test
3.   Question 3 in this test
4.   Question 4 in this test
5.   Question 5 in this test
6.   Question 6 in this test
7.   Question 7 in this test
8.   Question 8 in this test

List B
(a) Multiple choice
(b) Matching list
(c) Rearrangement
(d) Assertion/reason
(e) Short answer
(f) True/false
(g) Multiple response
(h) Sentence completion

Answer
1. matches with letter . . . .
2. matches with letter . . . .
3. matches with letter . . . .
4. matches with letter . . . .
5. matches with letter . . . .
6. matches with letter . . . .
7. matches with letter . . . .
8. matches with letter . . . .

Q7. STATEMENT 1
Objective testing fits with a behaviourist view of learning.

BECAUSE

STATEMENT 2
Items in an objective test have only one correct predetermined answer.

If you think both Statement 1 and Statement 2 are false, tick A
If you think Statement 1 is false and Statement 2 is true, tick B
If you think Statement 1 is true and statement 2 is false, tick C
If you think both statements are true but Statement 1 is not the reason for Statement 2, tick D
If you think both statements are true but Statement 1 is the reason for Statement 2, tick E

Answer
A   B   C   D   E

Q8. A. Behaviourists use closed questions as an assessment strategy.
B. S-R bonds are strengthened through reinforcement.
C. An aim describes the outcome expected of a learner.

If you think A, B and C are all correct, tick A
If you think A, B and C are all incorrect, tick B
If you think A and B are correct, but C is incorrect, tick C
If you think B and C are correct, but A is incorrect, tick D
If you think C is correct, but A and B are incorrect, tick E

Answer
A   B   C   D   E

You have hopefully answered all of the questions correctly (you can check your answers at the end of the chapter) and now can identify eight different types of objective item, noting that for each, there is only one possible correct answer.

REFLECTIVE TASK

Do you notice any difference in what is required of you in the first two questions as opposed to the remaining questions?
What do you see as the advantages and limitations of objective testing?

Objective items fall into two categories. Supply items require the respondent to provide the answer and thus test recall. This is a more demanding response than that required by the more common selection items, which test not recall, but recognition. In the above example, the first two questions are examples of supply items whereas the remaining questions ask you to select the correct answer from the options provided.

There are many arguments for and against objective testing. Criticisms include being too open to scoring through guessing and only assessing lower levels of learning.

Guessing applies particularly to selection items. In Question 6, for instance, you may not have known the answers but were still able to come up with the correct response. In this instance, you may have arrived at your response by a process of elimination and deduction rather than guesswork. In question 4, however, the multiple-choice question, respondents have a one in four chance of arriving at the correct answer through guesswork alone. In theory, someone who knew nothing about the subject could get a mark of 25 per cent in a test composed entirely of multiple choice questions with four options, perhaps more if they are lucky guessers. The True/False strategy provides an even greater chance of success. It is possible to counteract guessing through penalising incorrect answers and a number of different guessing corrections can be applied with varying degrees of success. Steps can be taken then, to minimise the effect of guessing but it remains impossible to factor out guessing completely.

It is possible, however, to assess higher levels of learning than just recall and recognition. Categorisations of levels of learning are usually based upon Benjamin Bloom's taxonomy of educational objectives, in which he identifies different levels of performance within each of the three domains of learning identified earlier in this chapter. Within the cognitive domain Bloom identifies the following levels.

KNOWLEDGE – Familiarity with the specific facts, terminology and principles of the subject. Typical objective:

> *by the end of this session, each learner will be able to* state *the six levels of Bloom's taxonomy in the cognitive domain*

COMPREHENSION – An understanding of and an ability to interpret subject matter. Typical objective:

> *by the end of this session, each learner will be able to* explain *why an action verb is required for a SMART objective*

APPLICATION – Being able to use the material learned in a given situation. Typical objective:

> *by the end of this session, each learner will be able to* use *learning objectives as a basis for lesson planning*

ANALYSIS – Breaking material down into constituent parts to find the relationship between them. Typical objective:

> *by the end of this session, each learner will be able to* compare and contrast *behaviourist and cognitive views of learning*

SYNTHESIS – Rethinking learned material to come up with a new idea or different perspective. Typical objective:

> *by the end of this session, each learner will be able to* design *a lesson based on behaviourist principles*

EVALUATION – To arrive at an informed judgment. Typical objective:

> *by the end of this session, each learner will be able to* constructively criticise *the behavioural approach to learning*

It can be seen that the taxonomy is hierarchical in nature. We cannot apply a principle, for instance, unless we know what it involves and comprehend what it means. We cannot evaluate the same principle unless we can analyse it or break it down into its constituent parts and then reconstruct or synthesise it in a way that shows we understand the relationship between those constituent parts. It is worth noting that the evaluation of teaching, which many managers and teachers are routinely asked to do, is a high-order skill which involves a number of sub-skills.

Returning to the objective test above, assessment has taken place largely at the lower end of Bloom's taxonomy – knowledge, comprehension and, arguably, application. This does not mean that the higher levels cannot be assessed through objective testing, as multiple response and assertion/reason items in particular can be designed to achieve this purpose. Generally, however, it is in assessing these lower levels that objective testing is used.

Objective testing does have two big advantages over other forms of testing and these lie in the areas of reliability and validity, both essential considerations in any form of assessment.

The results of any assessment should give a true indication of the actual ability of the person assessed. They should not be influenced by the conditions under which the assessment takes place or by the perceptions or opinions of whoever marks the assessment. The key to achieving this lies in consistency of both administration and marking of the assessment. The more consistency that can be achieved in the marking process, the higher the reliability of the ensuing results. There are a number of factors which influence reliability but the greatest of these is the degree of subjectivity exhibited by the marker. In an objective test, each item has only one correct answer so the issue of subjectivity on the part of the marker does not arise. As Child (2007, p519) remarks, *They are called 'objective' because the questions and answers are carefully predetermined, rendering the responses free from the personal biases of the examiner.* Many objective tests are actually marked by computer or machine rather than by human hand, giving rise to absolute consistency and removing marker subjectivity altogether. Objective testing gives results with a high degree of reliability.

Validity is concerned with the ability of the assessment to truly test what it sets out to test. Content validity is one form of validity and here the concern is with the amount of the syllabus that the assessment samples. The greater the coverage of syllabus of the assessment, the higher the content validity of the results. Some forms of assessment such as essays, while giving a deeper treatment of the chosen topic for assessment, are limited in the scope of their syllabus coverage. Objective tests with their sharper, shorter approach can effectively cover a wide range of syllabus topics, leading to results with high content validity.

There are then, a number of strengths and limitations associated with objective testing but regardless of how these are perceived, objective testing is the assessment method which is best suited to a behavioural view of learning.

The learning to be tested may not be knowledge-based, but rather a physical skill like plastering a wall or performing some kind of electrical installation. An objective test will be of limited use in this case as it would test only the knowledge required to perform the skill rather than the actual skill itself. This raises the issue of another type of validity – construct validity – which is concerned with whether or not the assessment method used actually tests the ability we wish it to. As we are now considering the 'doing' part of the skill, an objective test would be an inappropriate assessment method to use as it measures the 'knowing part' of the skill. To produce results with a high degree of construct validity we would need to use observation as our assessment method.

If the skill is reasonably complex in nature, it is likely that it will have been learned not as a single activity but instead will have been broken down into a series of stages and learned in a step-by-step fashion. All of these smaller steps contribute to the skill as a whole and therefore need to be taken into consideration when assessment takes place. It would be normal therefore, to use a checklist when observing a skill, the checklist itemising the different steps that contribute to the overall skill. Each stage of the skill would be marked accordingly. This also greatly increases the reliability of the results obtained by making the marking of the observation more objective.

Classroom management

When it comes to the issue of classroom management, it will by now have become apparent that the focus for the behaviourist is not the individual who is displaying the behaviour to be addressed, but rather the behaviour itself. The methods employed are therefore aimed at influencing and controlling actual behaviours. The setting of ground rules falls into this category as these identify behaviours which are acceptable and those which are not. As with any rule-based approach, strategies to encourage compliance then have to be put into place. These will normally involve punishment and the different types of reinforcement which were explored in the previous chapter, as these are the means through which behaviourists hope to influence what people do.

REFLECTIVE TASK

Of the two approaches – reinforcement and punishment – which do you consider to provide the most effective approach to classroom management? Can you see any potential problems with either?

With regard to the two options of reinforcement and punishment, punishment is regarded as the least effective for a number of reasons.

- Punishment may give rise to feelings of anxiety, fear, anger or resentment in the recipient which can exacerbate rather than solve behavioural problems.
- Punishment generally has only a temporary effect.
- If the undesirable behaviour is attention seeking, punishment can provide reinforcement, thus actually strengthening rather than eradicating it.

The main concern, however, is that punishment tells whoever is on the receiving end what not to do but does not inform them about what they should do. As a consequence, punishment can lead to the replacement of one undesirable behaviour by another.

Programmes of behaviour modification thus normally start by identifying what are deemed as acceptable behaviours, making these the focus. If these behaviours are seen, they are rewarded in some way – they are positively reinforced. Behaviours which fall outside of those which are regarded as acceptable are ignored on the basis that if they go unrewarded, they will eventually disappear altogether (extinction). The accent then, is on positively reinforcing the behaviours that are to be encouraged.

A variation on this theme is assertive discipline first introduced in America by Lee Canter (1979, 2001). Assertive discipline is a system of behaviour management which relies upon the consistent reinforcement of a limited number of clear, concise rules. Desirable behaviours are rewarded and undesirable behaviours lead to predetermined consequences. The assumption behind this approach is that generally, there is no acceptable reason for inappropriate behaviour. If learners know what is expected of them through the establishment of rules and procedures, reinforcement of these on a consistent basis will lead to effective classroom management. Such an approach clearly has behaviourist overtones but the concept of assertive discipline has evolved since its original inception into a form that is now rather less authoritarian and intends that learners, to a large extent, self-regulate their own behaviour.

The three aspects to the approach are:

1. rules which are to be followed at all times;
2. positive reinforcement when rules are followed;
3. consequences that result from not following the rules.

Rules are best kept to few in number (about five) and identify expected behaviours only, not academic matters. They are phrased in observable terms to avoid ambiguity and uncertainty and one way of arriving at a common understanding is to involve learners in devising the rules.

Consequences exist in a hierarchy dependent upon the nature, frequency and severity of the offence but importantly are deemed to result from a choice that the learner makes. Learners can make the choice of engaging in the expected, desirable behaviours, leading to positive reinforcement. Alternatively they can choose not to behave in this manner but the result of this choice is the acceptance of the resulting consequence, normally some form of sanction or punishment. If, however, the sanction or punishment leads to the desirable behaviour, it can be lifted, thus employing negative reinforcement to strengthen the desired behaviour.

If, for example, a learner does not follow a rule concerning talking while the teacher is talking, a sanction of staying on at the end of the session is applied as the agreed consequence. If the learner is now quiet for the remainder of the session, thus showing the desired behaviour, the sanction is lifted. The lifting of the sanction is an example of negative reinforcement and serves to strengthen the behaviour of not talking at the same time as the teacher. The above example is school-based in nature and this is where this approach is most commonly encountered, as a survey of the websites of different schools will confirm.

REFLECTIVE TASK

While the strategies of assertive discipline outlined above might work well in a school setting, can you envisage any instances where they might equally well be applied within the lifelong learning sector?

One of the aims of lifelong learning is to provide a different atmosphere from that encountered in the school environment, particularly if learners see it as their 'second chance' and perhaps many in the sector would see assertive discipline as being inappropriate for their learners and the relationship they wish to build with them. This would not be an issue as far as behaviourism is concerned as its focus is external to the person, but as teachers we would hopefully adopt a considerably less narrow viewpoint. Perhaps there are elements of assertive discipline which could be adapted or used, particularly in further education which recruits younger learners, as the impact of the 14–19 Education and Skills White Paper of 2005 is being increasingly felt. There are of course alternative approaches to classroom management and some of these will be encountered in later chapters.

A SUMMARY OF **KEY POINTS**

> **Behaviourists plan round learning objectives, which identify an action or observable behaviour which defines the learning that is to take place. These need to be written in a manner that is both specific and measurable and normally conform to a SMART format.**

> The formulation of objectives allows a systematic approach to planning to be adopted.

> The behaviourist principles of giving information in small chunks which are subsequently reinforced is used in programmed and computer-assisted approaches to learning.

> Behaviourist approaches employ closed questions either to assess learning or to provide a more parti-cipative way of building knowledge in a step-by-step fashion.

> Practical skills contain both a 'knowledge' and 'doing' component. Demonstration is used to transmit the 'knowledge' component and should be informed by a process of skills analysis.

> The 'doing' component is achieved by practice which is reinforced through external feedback.

> Knowledge is assessed by objective tests as these have only one predetermined correct answer. Objective tests can contain a number of different items. Skills are assessed by observation using a checklist which itemises the different components of the skill.

> Classroom management is achieved through the use of ground rules. Reinforcement techniques are applied in the process of assertive discipline.

Answers to practical tasks

From the list below, tick the words you might use to write SMART objectives.

The words denoted by * describe an 'observable behaviour' and therefore make good action verbs for a SMART objective. The remainder are processes that take place in the mind and are therefore unsuitable as action verbs.

define	*	choose	*	describe	*	differentiate between	*
state	*	appreciate		calculate	*	identify	*
report	*	list	*	understand		know	
comprehend		perform	*	sympathise with		explain	*
recognise	*	be aware of		classify	*	draw	*
select	*	sort	*	demonstrate	*	be conscious of	

Objective test on behaviourism

Q1 Operant
Q2 stimulus, response, reinforcer
Q3 FALSE
Q4 c
Q5 c, e, a, d, b
Q6 1e, 2h, 3f, 4a, 5c, 6b, 7d, 8g
Q7 E
Q8 C

REFERENCES REFERENCES **REFERENCES** REFERENCES **REFERENCES** REFERENCES

Bloom, B (1956) *Taxonomy of educational objectives*. Boston: Allyn and Bacon.

Canter, L (1979) Discipline: You can do it! *Instructor*, 89 (2): 106–12.

Canter, L and M (2001) *Assertive discipline: Positive behavior management for today's classroom* (3rd edn). Santa Monica: Canter and Associates.

Child, D (2007) *Psychology and the teacher* (8th edn). New York: Continuum International Publishing Group.

Fitts, P and Posner, M (1968) *Human performance.* New Jersey: Prentice Hall.

Francis, M and Gould, J (2009) *Achieving your PTTLS qualification: A practical guide to duccessful teaching in the lifelong learning sector*. London: Sage.

Gray, D, Griffin, C and Nasta, T (2000) *Training to teach in further and adult education*. Cheltenham: Stanley Thornes.

Hillier, Y (2005) *Reflective teaching in further and adult education*. London: Continuum.

Mager, RF (1975) *Preparing instructional objectives* (2nd edn). Belmont: Fearon Publishers Inc.

Marsh, CJ (2004) *Key concepts for understanding curriculum* (3rd edn). Abingdon: RoutledgeFalmer.

Prideaux, D (2000) The emperor's new clothes: From objectives to outcomes. *Medical Education*, 34: 168–9.

Race, P (2005) *Making learning happen: A guide for post-compulsory education*. London: Sage.

Tyler, RW (1949) *Basic principles of curriculum and instruction*. University of Chicago Press.

Walklin, L (1982) *Instructional techniques and practice*. Cheltenham: Stanley Thornes.

4
Cognitive approaches

Chapter overview and objectives

This chapter explores cognitive views on learning, comparing them with the behaviourist perspective outlined in Chapter 2. Cognitive is an umbrella term for several different approaches but all share the common feature of looking for meaning and understanding. Comparison with behaviourism will be made easier by providing answers to the same issues previously considered in Chapter 2, although not necessarily in the same order.

When you have worked through this chapter you will be able to:

- **recognise the strengths and limitations of the behaviourist perspective on learning;**
- **state the defining characteristics of the cognitive perspective on learning;**
- **describe the contribution of Gestalt psychology to an understanding of the learning process;**
- **define learning from a cognitive perspective and identify its source of motivation;**
- **differentiate between the approaches to learning advocated by Bruner and Ausubel;**
- **compare behaviourist and cognitive perspectives on learning.**

This chapter contributes to the following values and areas of professional knowledge as contained in the LLUK professional standards for teachers, tutors and trainers in the lifelong learning sector:

AS4, BS2, CS4, DS3

AK1.1, AK4.1, AK4.3, BK1.1, BK1.2, BK1.3, BK2.1, BK2.7, CK3.1

Cognitivism as a reaction to behaviourism

The last two chapters have dealt in some detail with behaviourism and how this particular perspective on learning can be translated into practice. Behaviourism was the major influence on educational practice in the 1960s and 1970s and it is clear that there are some distinct advantages in using this approach to teaching and learning.

Behaviourism introduced precision into the teaching and learning process, moving the emphasis away from content and towards the learning that was to take place. This precision and shift of emphasis allowed for a more accurate and exacting assessment process, an important consideration in a time of movement towards increased accountability in education. Furthermore, the 'scientific' approach upon which behaviourism was based, led easily into a systematic approach to planning.

REFLECTIVE TASK

The advantages of the objective approach, as outlined above, lie in its systematic nature, lack of ambiguity and ease of measurement. Can you identify any drawbacks to this approach? Can you identify any aspect of your current teaching where a behaviourist approach is unsuitable?

Despite bringing much-needed clarity to curriculum planning, behaviourism became the subject of considerable criticism, partly due to the style of teaching it encouraged and partly because it could not explain a number of different aspects of learning. As far as teaching style was concerned, the two main objections concerned the autocratic, teacher-led style behaviourism encouraged and the passive role taken by learners. The setting of objectives was undertaken by teachers who took guidance in this task from the needs of the syllabus and the requirements of the appropriate awarding body. The needs of learners were of secondary importance, if indeed they were addressed at all. Teaching tended to be centred on transmission-based methods and were designed to bring about an identical outcome on the part of all learners. Learners thus had no control over their own learning. The passive view taken of learners took no account of their independent and enquiring natures, which led some critics to argue that behaviourism was in fact a form of indoctrination and thus in conflict with the whole concept of education.

The second strand of objection involved the learning of subjects that are less to do with information or facts but are more conceptual and encompass controversy, debate and creativity. By their nature, such subjects do not readily lend themselves to an approach which defines in advance, the learning that is to take place. This is an issue to be explored further in the next chapter. The fundamental objection to behaviourism, however, lay in its attempt to reduce a complex process such as learning into a relatively simplistic framework which cannot account for many aspects of learning. It is these apparent flaws in behaviourism which led to the rise in popularity of the cognitive perspective on learning.

Amsel (1989, p1) is often quoted to illustrate this tension between the two approaches and the challenge that behaviourism now faced:

> *I like to point out that the S–R psychologists, who at one time formed the government, are now in loyal opposition, the cognitivists being the new government.*

The cognitive perspective emphasises meaning and understanding as opposed to the more mechanistic viewpoint adopted by behaviourists.

Consider for example, the following passage:

> *Aoccdrnig to rscheearch at Cmabrigde Uinervtisy, it deosn't mttaer in waht oredr the ltteers in a wrod are, the olny iprmoetnt tihng is taht the frist and lsat ltteer be at the rghit pclae. The rset can be a toatl mses and you can sitll raed it wouthit porbelm. Tihs is bcuseae the huamn mnid deos not raed ervey lteter by istlef, but the wrod as a wlohe.*

Does it make sense to you? If you were a behaviourist the likely answer would be *no*. The research at Cambridge, however, suggests it does make sense and you will undoubtedly have agreed with its conclusion. But how did you arrive at an understanding of this passage? When you looked at the first word *Aoccdrnig* by itself, it will have been fairly meaningless. When you viewed it in conjunction with the next two words, *Aoccdrnig to rscheearch*, however, it began to make sense. Why is this the case and more to the point, why did you bother to persevere in trying to understand the passage? The answers to these questions tell us a lot about the nature of learning from a cognitive perspective and this approach to learning is the concern of this chapter.

General cognitive principles

Cognitive theories are concerned with what happens inside our heads as we learn. They maintain that information is actively processed and learning takes place by organising and finding the relationships that exist between different pieces of information. Cognitive approaches do not come under the heading of a single theory but consist of a number of different strands. Best (1995) classifies these as 'connectionist' theories, which focus on the brain and its neural connections and 'information processing' theories – those which argue that the mind works like a computer. Each offers a rather different viewpoint and approach.

Fundamental to all cognitive approaches, however, are the concepts of meaning and under-standing and the internalisation of the process of learning. Eysenck and Keane (2005, p1) offer the following definition:

> It [cognitive psychology] is concerned with the internal processes involved in making sense of the environment, and deciding what action might be appropriate.

This differs from behaviourism in that it is less concerned with the actual stimulus and resulting response but focuses more on what happens in between these two events; how an action is arrived at through the interpretation and processing of the initial stimulus. Learning is thus a process internal to the individual rather than an automatic response to an external event. These internal processes lie at the heart of the cognitive approach and are described as mediating processes or more simply, mediators, as they come between the stimulus and the response. It is the different perceptions of these mediators that give rise to the variety within cognitive theory.

Although there are different strands to cognitive theory, they are all underpinned by a number of common assumptions. Foremost in these is the belief that learning builds upon previous experience. This means that in order to have meaning, new learning must be able to be related to previous learning and experience, which in turn influences the interpretation we place on new learning.

Meaning depends upon relationships and there are a number of strategies used to establish what these relationships are.

Schema

A schema is a mental category or structure which contains the knowledge and experience we possess about something. As our knowledge and experience increase, so the schema changes and becomes more complex to accommodate this. According to Piaget, this is how cognitive development takes place. Combinations of schema (or schemata as it is in the plural), form cognitive structures which we use to interpret and understand the world.

Scripts

There are many different types of schemata, of which a script is one. In a restaurant, the waiter will act and behave differently to a customer as each will have a different script to guide their actions. Scripts are the schemata employed to interpret and guide action in social situations.

Scaffolding

When a building is in its early stages of construction, scaffolding is essential to allow work to progress. The nearer the building comes to completion, however, the less the scaffolding is needed and it is eventually dispensed with altogether. Similarly, the construction of a schema may require some form of support. A teacher will help a child, for instance, by giving initial support and guidance by using a variety of strategies such as telling, questioning and demonstrating. They will gradually reduce their level of support, however, as learning occurs, until eventually, as with the building, support is no longer needed. This process is also known as scaffolding.

In general then, a cognitive perspective suggests that:

- current learning builds upon previous learning;
- learning involves deriving understanding and meaning;
- meaning is dependent upon establishing relationships;
- relationships are stored internally as cognitive structures.

REFLECTIVE TASK

In the previous reflective task, you were asked to identify any aspect of your current teaching where a behaviourist approach is unsuitable. Is a cognitive approach likely to be more appropriate in the instances you identified?

Are there any other aspects of your current teaching which might fall into this category? Use the four characteristics of a cognitive approach listed above to help you arrive at your decisions.

One approach that falls under the heading of cognitive theory is that of Gestalt psychology. Returning for a moment to the earlier passage on reading, the researchers at Cambridge suggested that you were able to make sense of the passage because you looked at the word as a whole rather than considering every letter by itself. An extension of that argument suggests that the individual words may have made no sense on their own but when viewed as part of a bigger phrase or sentence, meaning emerged. A similar situation arises when listening to a piece of orchestral music. Listening to each individual instrument in isolation would not be very rewarding but when all the instruments are heard together, the piece of music takes on a whole new meaning. These two examples illustrate the Gestalt motto, which states that 'the whole is greater than the sum of its parts'.

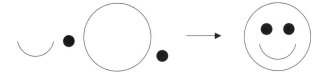

Defining learning from a cognitive perspective

According to Gestalt psychology then, in order to have meaning, learning must encompass the whole picture as this reveals the relationship between the individual parts. The analogy of a jigsaw is useful in seeing how this relates to learning.

The individual bits of a jigsaw puzzle have, in themselves, no particular meaning. As we fit the pieces together, however, a picture begins to emerge. As a new piece is added, our understanding of the picture changes a little and when the final piece falls into place, the jigsaw takes on meaning for us as we can see the whole picture and how the pieces of the jigsaw relate to each other in forming this picture.

So it is with learning. Individual items of information have limited meaning in themselves and so accumulating more and more knowledge does not constitute learning. This is analogous to filling up the jigsaw box with more and more pieces. The knowledge gained only constitutes learning when we can relate it to and see how it fits with the bigger picture that we already possess (our previous knowledge and experience). When we have established this fit, the bigger picture, or our understanding, has changed as a result. It has taken on a new meaning and so learning has taken place. In the language of psychology, the way in which the different items of information fit together to form a meaningful whole is known as a cognitive structure. As new bits of related information are received, the cognitive structure changes in form to accommodate them. From a cognitive perspective, learning can thus be defined as:

> a change in cognitive structures; the way in which we perceive events and organise experiences to arrive at understanding.

How does this process take place? One of the earliest challenges to behaviourism came from Wolfgang Koehler, who, in his book *The mentality of apes* (1925) argued that we tend to organise knowledge and experience in a specific manner and this occurs through a process of insight. Koehler claimed that his experiments with chimpanzees provided examples of insight. One such experiment concerned Sultan the chimpanzee. Sultan had to use a stick to reach a banana placed outside the bars of his cage, out of arm's reach. He had learned to use the stick to pull the banana close enough to the cage so that he could pick it up. Koehler then moved the banana further away from the cage so it could not be reached with the short stick but also placed a longer stick outside the cage, but out of the immediate reach of Sultan. Sultan tried to retrieve the banana with the shorter stick and after several unsuccessful attempts, retreated to the back of the cage in frustration. Some time later, he suddenly went to the shorter stick, used it to pull the longer stick towards the cage and into reach, and then retrieved the banana with the longer stick.

Koehler's explanation of this sequence of events was that Sultan had reorganised the elements of the situation in his mind to arrive at a solution to the problem. The elements required to solve the problem had always been present but only when the appropriate relationship between them was identified did they have any meaning in the context of the problem itself. Learning was thus achieved through insight. Popularly known as 'the penny drops' or the 'aha' moment, this phenomenon was even more dramatically demonstrated by Archimedes, who was in his bathtub when he solved the puzzle of the purity of the gold used to make the King's crown and then famously, ran naked through the streets of Syracuse shouting *eureka* (I have found it!) to tell the king of his discovery. From a Gestalt perspective then, learning is the understanding of a subject as a whole and takes place through a process of insight.

> Learning is a complex activity in which the learner relates each new perception to the whole of his/her previous experience. As a result, the learner gains insight.

Sources of motivation

We have previously discussed reward and punishment as sources of motivation. Undoubtedly these will have an effect both on you and on those you teach. Are they the only sources of motivation or can you identify others that you respond to?

Gestalt psychologists have identified a number of strategies, known as the laws of pragnanz, that are used to impose some kind of pattern or meaning on what we see and the experiences we have. One of these is known as closure. Consider the drawings below.

What do you think they are?

The chances are that your response is that they are the letters E and T. In fact, they are a series of unconnected lines. In a cognitive world, however, we strive to find meaning in what we see and experience, so a series of unrelated lines create a tension or curiosity that can only be relieved by finding the meaning we seek. To achieve this, we mentally add the missing parts to the picture, or close the gaps and see the whole picture.

Similarly, th_ s_nt_nce I _m typ_n_ now makes sense to you although it is incomplete. You may find that when you are having a conversation with someone, you tend to finish off their sentences for them. While irritating, this also serves as another example of closure, where we are mentally racing ahead of the words we hear in order to establish meaning. This is a powerful urge and tells us something of the nature of motivation within a cognitive approach. Closure is a result of the need to attribute meaning. Without meaning, a psychological tension exists – it is an itch which must be scratched. Bruner described this phenomenon as *curiosity drive* whilst Piaget used the term *intellectual disturbance*. Whatever label is used, in a cognitive view of learning, motivation is internal to the person and stems from the need to find meaning. Only when meaning has been established can satisfaction be achieved.

> *In a cognitive approach to learning, motivation is derived intrinsically as individual needs are satisfied. It is the result of curiosity or a need to find meaning.*

Piaget (1896–1980) was one of the earliest and most influential cognitivists. He developed the idea that children make sense of and come to an understanding of their interactions with their environment through the building of cognitive structures which increase in sophistication and complexity as the child develops. Piaget maintained that this occurs as a series of four developmental stages, starting with simple reflexes and gradually building up to complex mental activity. Piaget related these developmental stages to the child's age, the first of these, known as the sensori-motor stage, covering the age range of 0 to 2 years old and the last, formal operations, occurring from 11 years onwards.

With respect to lifelong learning, however, the views of Jerome Bruner, who built on Piaget's work, and David Ausubel are more pertinent.

Ausubel and Bruner are both cognitivists and therefore subscribe to the same basic underpinning principles of the cognitive approach. Both agree that new learning builds on existing learning, that understanding and meaning are paramount in learning and that meaning is dependent upon establishing relationships. They both agree that to achieve this, knowledge must be structured and organised. Where they differ is in their views on where that structure should come from – teachers or learners.

Meaningful reception learning

Ausubel (1963) suggests a model where information is presented to learners in an organised manner. His argument is that if the organisation of learned material is required in order for meaningful learning to take place, then this is the form in which it should initially be presented to learners. The *tell them what you are going to tell them, tell them, tell them what you have told them* mantra is based around Ausubel's approach. Meaningful learning is key to this process. Meaningful learning, according to Ausubel, entails acquiring new knowledge that links to existing knowledge and which can subsequently be easily retained and applied. Ausubel considers knowledge to be hierarchically organised and that new information is meaningful only to the extent that it can be related to what is already known.

This integration of new knowledge into existing structures is known as subsumption and forms the basis of Ausubel's approach. He calls this type of learning meaningful reception learning, and is at pains to distinguish it from rote learning, which he contends is not meaningful as the appropriate links between existing and new knowledge are not being made. Ausubel also stresses the active nature of meaningful reception learning as opposed to its passive behaviourist counterpart of rote learning.

Ausubel suggests that a teaching session should start with an 'advance organiser'. This is information that is presented prior to learning taking place and its function is to put learners in the frame of mind which will allow them to interpret and organise the new information presented in the desired manner, thus achieving meaningful learning. An advance organiser is therefore a mechanism for linking new information with existing knowledge and helps to present the big picture first before proceeding to examine the detail. In the above section on closure, if I had given the clue *go home* before you looked at the drawings this would have acted as an advance organiser.

REFLECTIVE TASK

From your own experience of learning, can you identify an advance organiser that has been used? Devise an advance organiser you could use in your own teaching

Discovery learning

In contrast to Ausubel, Bruner (1963) believed that when presented with information in a highly structured manner, learners become over-dependent on others. Learners should therefore be encouraged to discover information and its interrelationships for themselves as this would allow them to remember the information for a longer period of time and also increase their ability to apply new knowledge to real-life situations. This is a form of constructivism which centres on the belief that learning is derived or constructed by building upon and linking to existing previous learning. The teaching methods, such as problem-solving, which are associated with Bruner's viewpoint are discussed in the next chapter, but it can be seen that his view of learning contrasts sharply with the relatively passive, trans-mission-based methods discussed in the previous chapter. It is also evident that in a cognitive approach to learning, the learner is an active participant in the learning process, interacting with and organising the material to be learned.

Learning is an active process. The learner actively seeks stimuli, undertakes discovery learning, reorganising and restructuring the material to be learned.

Discovery learning then, as advocated by Bruner, takes place when the main content of the learning session is not provided by the teacher, but is independently arrived at by the learner. The learner is thus an active participant in their own learning and the role of the teacher becomes one of providing whatever is required in the way of structure, guidance and resources in order for 'discovery' to successfully take place. As discovery learning is based upon the learner's prior knowledge and experience, however, it cannot be assumed that all learners are at the same starting point or that they will interpret and understand everything in the same manner. Discovery learning therefore requires some individualisation and a sound knowledge of learners and their previous knowledge and experience.

REFLECTIVE TASK

Can you identify instances from your own experience of learning that have taken a discovery approach? How did you find this?

Identify one area within your own teaching that might benefit from a discovery-based approach to learning. How might you implement this approach?

Another of Bruner's major contributions to teaching and learning concerns sequencing. He built on Piaget's developmental stages and suggested that as children develop cognitively, they use three different ways, or modes, of making sense of the world they inhabit. These three modes of representation signify how information and knowledge are recognised, organised and subsequently stored. The names given to them are:

- enactive – learning is based around actions or objects;
- iconic – learning is based around images such as pictures, illustrations and models;
- symbolic – learning is based around language, number or other abstract symbolic representations.

Bruner suggests that in the cognitive development of children, the sequence followed is the enactive mode first, followed by the iconic and finally the symbolic mode. Most effective learning, however, does involve a combination of these three modes. This sequencing principle can be applied to all learners, regardless of age, and holds just as true for adult learners as for others. The sequence is to start from a concrete experience, illustrate visually and finally describe in words. The enactive mode is very much rooted in the real world whereas language and other symbolic representations work at the abstract level. The move-ment therefore is from the concrete to the abstract – a notion that will be explored further in the next chapter.

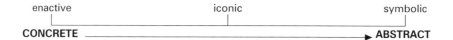

enactive   iconic   symbolic

CONCRETE ——————————————————————→ ABSTRACT

REFLECTIVE TASK

REFLECTIVE TASK

Which of the two approaches to learning described above (meaningful reception learning and discovery-based approaches) do you think best suits your learners and why do you think this is the case?

How is learning built up in a cognitive approach?

Learning is defined in this approach as a change in cognitive structures. Cognitive structures have been described as a way of mentally storing information in categories that make relationships clear. In behaviourism, learning was built up in a step-by-step manner taking 'bits' of information and adding them to others in a linear process. The nature of knowledge in a cognitive viewpoint is one in which the 'bits' of information are all interrelated and collectively have a specific meaning. When new information is taken in therefore, it becomes part of that larger picture but as a consequence, the picture changes.

Consider making a cup of coffee. Coffee granules are placed in the cup. How many items are in the cup? I think you will agree it is one. Water is now added and the mix stirred. How many items are in the cup? Is it one or is it two? Similarly, milk and sugar are added. Are there four items in the cup now or one? The answer is that there is always one item in the cup but it changes each time something else is added. This is analogous to learning when considered from a cognitive perspective. We have a particular view, picture or cognitive structure relating to a given subject. We now learn something new about this subject, but it is not merely another fact that is added to an existing repository of knowledge; it becomes part of what we know but in doing so alters our overall view of the subject. We now see it slightly differently as our picture or cognitive structure has undergone a change as a result of assimilating this new piece of knowledge. Rather than adding to the store, new knowledge transforms existing knowledge.

Learning is built up as each new piece of learning is integrated with what has been learned before, leading to a new and deeper understanding.

Learners become aware of this deeper understanding as it builds up; they recognise that they know more than they did before. There is an internal realisation that learning has taken place and there is no need to be informed of this by an external source either through feedback or reinforcement. If, for example, you have brought up children, you are aware that you now know far more about that process than you did when you first started out. If you were asked to itemise your knowledge on the subject, however, this may cause you some problems as that knowledge has gradually changed in form as your experience increased. Your view on bringing up children is that of the big picture rather than a series of facts. Nonetheless you could come up with a satisfactory response but it is unlikely you would compose your list in a random fashion. In all probability you would start off from one thought which would lead to another related thought, which in turn would identify the next, and so on as you revisited and identified the structure of your child-rearing schema.

Learning accumulates in such a way that the learner has a growing awareness of their own understanding and competence.

Transfer of learning

The importance of transfer of learning and the conditions which make this more likely were discussed in Chapter 2 using the examples of roller skating and ice skating to illustrate positive transfer, and water skiing and skiing on snow to demonstrate negative transfer. Chapter 2 suggested that because of the highly specific nature of behaviourism, transfer of learning is unlikely. Transfer is much more likely to occur when the initial learning involves not specific instances, but an understanding of underlying principles. Specific knowledge or skills can only transfer to situations with a close similarity to the original, whereas an understanding of basic principles can impact on a much wider range of instances.

Suppose you are shown how to comment on a piece of work in order to give feedback to the person who has submitted it. It is likely that you will be able to put that knowledge to good use when you next mark a piece of work, although if the original example was a well-written piece and the work you are now confronted with is of poor quality, it may be less useful. If on the other hand, you understand the general principles of giving effective feedback you would be able to use this knowledge in a variety of circumstances – written comment, spoken comment, to individuals or groups – irrespective of the quality of the work.

Bruner (1963, p25) suggests that *an understanding of fundamental principles and ideas... appears to be the main road to adequate 'transfer of training'* and *the more fundamental or basic is the idea he has learned, almost by definition, the greater will be its breadth of applicability to new problems* (1963, p18).

The kind of transfer identified above by Bruner is often described as 'high-road' transfer (Woolfolk, Hughes and Walkup, 2008, p385) which *involves consciously applying abstract knowledge or strategies learned in one situation to a different situation*. This contrasts with 'low-road' transfer, which allows far less generalisation and is reminiscent of behaviourism in that it *involves the spontaneous, automatic transfer of highly practical skills with little use for reflective thinking*.

Transfer is to be expected due to the grasping of principles and development of cognitive strategies.

This chapter has not covered all aspects of cognitive theory; information processing theory, for example, is an important aspect of cognitive theory and will feature in later chapters. It is evident from the theories that have been covered, however, that a cognitive approach to learning differs considerably from that suggested by the behaviourists.

PRACTICAL TASK PRACTICAL TASK PRACTICAL TASK PRACTICAL TASK PRACTICAL TASK

Complete the gaps in the table below to check your understanding of the two theories and how they compare to each other. Check your responses with the table at the end of the chapter.

Comparison of behaviourist and cognitive perspectives on learning

	Behaviourist perspective	Cognitive perspective
Definition of learning		
How learning occurs		
How learning is built up		
Active or passive?		
Source of motivation		
How the learner knows they have learned		
Likelihood of transfer		

You may have found this view of learning more challenging to understand than the behaviourist view expressed in Chapter 2, and had to go back and re-read some parts of this chapter to fully understand what has been said. It has proved more difficult to write. This reflects the abstract nature of the approach. It deals with processes that occur in the mind and are not visible or indeed accessible through any of the senses, and the language of cognitive psychology contains many metaphors and analogies which try to make it more concrete and subsequently accessible.

Each of the two perspectives examined so far, however, makes its own contribution to an understanding of practice, and both have a place in any consideration of the process of teaching and learning. The next chapter looks at the implications of a cognitive perspective for practice in the shape of planning, methods, assessment and classroom management and you should find that these contrast quite sharply with the practice outlined in Chapter 3.

A SUMMARY OF **KEY POINTS**

> Perceived shortcomings in behaviourism (reductionism, prescription and transmission-based teaching methods) contributed to increased support for the cognitive perspective on learning.

> Cognitive theory is concerned with internal mental processes which seek understanding and meaning in the material to be learned.

> Meaning is derived from relating new learning to existing learning. This is achieved through the use of internal cognitive structures such as schema and scripts.

> Gestalt theory suggests that viewing the whole picture rather than its constituent parts leads to the establishment of meaning.

> Learning takes place when change is brought about in cognitive structures as a result of the need to accommodate and integrate new learning. This process is known as insight.

> Motivation is intrinsic, stemming from curiosity and a need to establish meaning.

> Ausubel suggests that meaning and structure should be established first in any new episode of learning.

> Bruner is of the opinion that learning is more effective when structure and meaning are discovered through the learner's own efforts.

> Learning is an active process involving direct engagement with the material to be learned.

> New learning leads to a greater and deeper understanding resulting in increased awareness in the learner.

> Cognitive learning involves an understanding of general principles and this increases the likelihood of transfer of learning.

Answer to practical task

Comparison of Behaviourist and Cognitive perspectives on learning

	Behaviourist perspective	Cognitive perspective
Definition of learning	Learning is a permanent change in behaviour resulting from some form of activity or experience	Learning is a change in cognitive structures; the way in which we perceive events, organise experiences, solve problems
How learning occurs	The change in behaviour comes about as a result of the establishment of a simple stimulus – response pattern	Learning occurs through insight as the learner relates each new perception to the whole of their previous experience
How learning is built up	Learning is built up by a step-by-step process	Each new piece of learning is integrated with and transforms previous learning
Active or passive?	Generally regarded as a relatively passive form of learning.	The learner seeks out stimuli, and engages in active thought processes
Source of motivation	Motivation is controlled extrinsically by reward or punishment	Motivation is derived intrinsically as individual needs are satisfied
How the learner knows they have learned	Immediate knowledge of results is important. The required response is reinforced by successful performance, especially if this is rewarded	Learning accumulates in such a way that the learner has a growing awareness of their own understanding and competence.
Likelihood of transfer	Transfer is limited and only occurs when two situations are very similar	Transfer is to be expected due to grasping of principles and development of cognitive strategies

REFERENCES REFERENCES **REFERENCES** REFERENCES REFERENCES REFERENCES

Amsel, A (1989) *Behaviourism, neobehaviourism and cognitivism in learning theory; historical and contemporary perspectives*. New Jersey: Erlbaum.

Ausubel, D (1963) *The psychology of meaningful verbal learning*. New York: Grune and Stratton.

Best, J, (1995) *Cognitive psychology* (4th edn). Minneapolis: West Group.

Bruner, J (1963) *The Process of Education.* Cambridge, Mass.: Harvard University Press.

Eysenck, MW and Keane, MT (2005) *Cognitive psychology, a student's handbook* (5th edn). East Sussex: Psychology Press.

Koehler, W (1925) *The mentality of apes.* New York: Harcourt and Brace.

Woolfolk A, Hughes, M and Walkup, V (2008) *Psychology in education*. Harlow: Pearson Education.

5

Implications of cognitive approaches for practice

Chapter overview and objectives

This chapter considers the implications of cognitive theory for practice. Generally, planning must be of a flexible and open nature as learning seeks to achieve understanding and derive individual meaning. Teaching methods need to establish the structure of what is being learned and this requires learners to take on an active role and engage with the material to be learned. Assessment also takes on its own particular form, as to produce valid results it must look for reasoned argument rather than correct answers. The chapter ends with discussion of an approach to classroom management which focuses not on behaviour in isolation, but rather looks for solutions by a consideration of the whole person of whom that behaviour is only one part.

When you have worked through this chapter you will be able to:

- **identify the significant features of the planning process in a cognitive approach to learning;**
- **differentiate between product and process models of curriculum;**
- **manage discussion as a learning activity in line with cognitive principles;**
- **distinguish between inductive and deductive approaches to learning, identifying the significant features of each;**
- **identify the steps in a systematic approach to problem-solving and use these to manage problem solving activities in a non-directive manner;**
- **describe how mind maps are constructed and how they illustrate a cognitive approach to learning;**
- **recognise assessment methods which are appropriate to a cognitive view of learning;**
- **describe the range of attributes that can be assessed by an essay;**
- **explain the role of academic self-concept in determining behaviour in a learning environment;**
- **identify strategies for classroom management which derive from a cognitive perspective.**

This chapter contributes to the following values and areas of professional knowledge as contained in the LLUK professional standards for teachers, tutors and trainers in the lifelong learning sector:

AS4, BS2, CS4, DS3

Planning from a cognitive perspective

The previous chapter noted the significant features of a cognitive approach as:

- the search for meaning and understanding;
- the need to relate new learning to existing learning to achieve such meaning;

- a consideration of the whole picture and the relationship between the constituent parts;
- the individual ways of organising and structuring the material to be learned.

REFLECTIVE TASK
BEETECTIVE TASK

Given that a cognitive view of learning is so different from a behaviourist view, how do you think planning will differ? Will the starting point be the same? Will it be as systematic? Think of an area of your teaching which involves the type of learning which a cognitive approach describes. How do you plan your teaching sessions in such circumstances?

Rather than individual bits of information, the cognitive approach seeks a consideration of the whole picture of what is to be learned and this needs to be reflected in the planning process. Relationships are key to understanding and so establishing these clearly and unambiguously is also an important consideration in planning how to present and structure the learning experience.

In terms of sequencing, Ausubel (1963) suggests that the most general ideas of a subject and the relationships they exemplify should be presented first and then be gradually broken down into more detail. Bruner's discovery-based approach aims for learners to arrive at the bigger picture through their own efforts, starting off from specific examples. Regardless, however, of whether Ausubel's more teacher-led approach or the more student-led approach suggested by Bruner is to be adopted, the teacher needs a clear image in their own mind of the structure and relationships involved in the material that learners will encounter. Without this, the material will not be presented to learners in a way that will make those relationships evident, or learning will not be structured in a manner that will easily facilitate the discovery of such relationships. Quite simply, you cannot teach understanding if you do not have it yourself, so highlighting and keeping this understanding at the forefront of the mind is the first stage in planning and preparation. While this may seem an obvious statement, take note of the story below, which is told by Bruner (1963, p89) of a college professor teaching an advanced class in quantum mechanics.

> *I went through it once and looked up only to find the class full of blank faces – they had obviously not understood. I went through it a second time and they still did not understand it. And so I went through it a third time, and that time I understood it.*

The second major area for consideration stems from the principle that, in order for meaning to be established, learners must be able to relate the material to be learned to their own prior knowledge and experience. Relevant previous knowledge and experience required must therefore be identified. More importantly, do learners possess this previous knowledge and experience, either collectively or individually, and is it sufficient to allow assimilation of the new material? As well as knowing their subject in a deep rather than surface manner, teachers adopting the cognitive approach must also know their learners sufficiently well to ensure that the most appropriate strategies are adopted to achieve a sound understanding of what is to be learned.

Turning to structure, it has been seen that learning objectives provide this in a very systematic way.

REFLECTIVE TASK

REFLECTIVE TASK

Do you think that learning objectives should be used to provide structure in a cognitive approach?

Suppose the subject to be taught was *an understanding of the causes of the First World War*. How would this be expressed in terms of learning objectives? Obviously the term 'understanding' could not be used to phrase the objectives as it is not an action verb. What would be required is a definition of what was meant by understanding in behavioural terms. The end result might look something like:

1. *List the different alliances that existed in Europe prior to the outbreak of war in 1914.*
2. *Identify the international tension in Europe caused by the 'scramble for Africa'.*
3. *State the reasons for the murder, in 1914, of Archduke Franz Ferdinand by Serbian nationalists.*

But if learners were to achieve these objectives, would they actually be exhibiting understanding? Would they be able to identify the relationships between these factors and show how one was dependent on or caused by another? Could they present a reasoned argument as to how these factors combined to cause war to break out? If the achievement of the above objectives was the sum total of the learning that took place, then this would not be the case.

It would appear then, that to establish structure in a teaching session based around a cognitive view of learning, learning objectives do not provide the solution as they are at odds with the type of learning that is to be achieved. Much learning is also spontaneous rather than planned and cannot be anticipated in advance, while other learning is creative in nature, seeking to arrive at new or novel solutions to problems. In both of these cases, learning objectives are unsuitable.

Learning objectives do not fit with a cognitive approach therefore, as they:

- focus only on behaviour;
- assume the identical outcome for each learner.

What is required is a type of objective that does not reduce learning to mechanistic behaviours and is sufficiently flexible to allow for some individual interpretation. A type of objective which fits this description, known as an expressive objective, has been suggested by Elliot Eisner (1969).

Eisner's background was in the field of art and the prescriptive, specific nature of behavioural, or instructional, objectives as he preferred to call them, was at odds with the more spontaneous and creative approach required in his subject area. He proposed, therefore, a different kind of objective, which he called an *expressive objective* which was *evocative rather than prescriptive*. These objectives describe an *educational encounter* rather than a prescription of what is to be learned.

> *It [expressive objective] identifies a situation in which children are to work, a problem with which they are to cope, a task in which they are to engage; but it*

does not specify what from that encounter, situation, problem, or task they are to learn.

(Eisner, 1969, pp15–16)

In setting an expressive objective,

the teacher hopes to provide a situation in which meanings become personalised and in which children produce products, both theoretical and qualitative, that are as diverse as themselves

(Eisner, 1969, p16)

Eisner suggests the following as examples of expressive objectives:

- to interpret the meaning of *Paradise Lost*;
- to examine and appraise the significance of *The Old Man and the Sea*;
- to develop a three-dimensional form through the use of wire and wood;
- to visit the zoo and discuss what was of interest there.

This approach is in keeping with both with cognitive learning theory and with its accompanying curriculum planning model – the process model. This contrasts with the product model of curriculum which you met in Chapter 3, which stems from behaviourist learning theory. The analogy of a journey is often used to distinguish between these two models of curriculum. The product model is often compared with a journey which has been carefully planned so to arrive at a given destination, whereas in the process model, reaching the destination is of less significance than what is learned along the way.

The main purpose of the process model of curriculum is to develop the intellect by focusing on the processes involved in thinking and reasoning. Different subjects involve key concepts and principles which form a network of relationships and to properly understand a subject, learners need to be familiar with both the subject's structure and its particular ways of thinking and proceeding, rather than accumulating a store of its facts and knowledge. As a result of being taught science for instance, learners should be able to think and act in a scientific manner. They should be 'scientists' rather than stores of science facts.

Bruner and Stenhouse were both advocates of the process approach and produced learning programmes (Bruner, 1965 – 'Man, a course of study'; Stenhouse, 1966 – 'The humanities curriculum project') which embodied its principles. In each, planning started not from a consideration of behavioural objectives but from a broad aim and the subsequent setting up of activities which encouraged learners to engage in enquiry, thinking and reasoning. This demands a specific role of the teacher variously described as 'senior learner' and 'problem-setter' rather than 'solution-giver'.

The process model of curriculum is not without its critics and limitations. In particular, it struggles for acceptance in the current educational climate of accountability because of its approach to assessment, which it considers to be developmental in nature. Stenhouse (1975, p95) states that *the teacher ought to be a critic, not a marker* and this means that:

It [the process model] can never be directed towards an examination as an objective without loss of quality, since the standards of the examination then override the standards immanent in the subject.

So, it can be seen that the process model of curriculum is based on cognitive learning theory assuming that each subject has its own ideas, concepts and structure. Its focus is on the process of thinking and how material is processed and organised. The contrast with the product model of curriculum, derived from behaviourist learning theory and based around the specification of objectives is detailed in the table below.

Product	Process
1. Based around behavioural objectives	1. Based around expressive objectives or activities
2. Closed, prescriptive in nature	2. Open-ended, outcomes unknown
3. Homogenous in outcome	3. Diversity in outcome
4. Focus on subject, tends to be teacher-led	4. Focus on learning, tends to be learner-led
5. Teacher considered to be expert	5. Teacher viewed as 'senior learner'
6. Assessment usually formal – summative in nature	6. Mutual evaluation rather than assessment – formative in nature
7. Tends to be associated with vocational courses	7. Tends to be associated with academic courses

Teaching methods

The methods of teaching appropriate to a cognitive approach will focus more on the learning process than the content and will have understanding as their goal. Learners will be encouraged to think, process and organise information in their own particular way rather than recall the same content as everyone else. Consequently, methods are generally more open than those encountered in a behaviourist approach and give a considerable amount of control to learners.

REFLECTIVE TASK

What type of teaching approaches do you think might encourage thinking, processing and organising information?

Discussion

Discussion is an activity in which opinions are shared and debated among participants. Assuming the activity is properly managed, all learners will participate fully in a common experience, and be exposed to the same arguments and points raised, but will take away their own individual conclusions and learning. For some, the learning achieved may well be similar but for others it may be quite different. For all, however, there will be an understanding of the result of their own learning and the relationship between all of the different factors which have contributed to it.

REFLECTIVE TASK

REFLECTIVE TASK

Think back to some past experience of taking part in some form of organised discussion where you may have learnt very little or even nothing at all. Jot down a few notes on why this was so and what could have been done to improve the situation. Now do the same for an effective discussion where you or group members learnt a lot, were successful, enjoyed it and were interested. What was it that made it an effective experience?

Careful management of any type of discussion is required if it is to achieve its desired effect. The more important aspects of managing discussions include the following.

Choice of topic

Discussion is most effective when there is a clear, agreed purpose in mind and a subject which lends itself to some form of deliberation. No matter how well managed otherwise, a discussion can fail due to inappropriate choice of topic. The chosen topic must be seen as relevant by learners if it is to draw them in and encourage participation. If too factual, there is little room for argument or debate and discussion will soon dry up, so the topic must be reasonably contentious as well as relevant, allowing scope for meaningful discussion and contribution.

Management of participants

Participation in discussion is more likely when everyone feels a part of the process and their contributions matter. This can be influenced directly by using questioning, positively acknowledging contributions and setting appropriate ground rules by which the discussion should operate. The use of verbal and non-verbal cues can also be used to encourage active listening and discourage a competitive atmosphere. Example, however, is just as important and although discussion may be a managed activity to some extent, learners have to feel that it is 'their' discussion. In a cognitive approach, the intention is that learners should arrive at their own conclusions, based on their own thought processes and so it is important that the teacher acts as what Stenhouse (1975, p39) terms a *neutral chairman*, not expressing or forcing their own views upon the discussion.

Management of process

A discussion can be organised in more than one way. It can be run as a whole-group activity or can be managed initially as a number of smaller groups. These smaller groups may all consider the main discussion topic or alternatively each may focus on different parts or perspectives of the main topic. Learners generally feel more at ease participating in smaller groups in the first instance and are more confident making contributions in a larger group having had time to consider the issues and had some confirmation of their thoughts from others. Having completed their tasks, the smaller groups would then normally come together to pool their thoughts and contribute to the bigger picture under consideration. Decisions have to be made as to which approach will be more suitable for the given occasion and if small groups are to be used, size, composition and exact task need careful consideration. If a whole-group approach is considered the more appropriate, it can be more difficult to initiate discussion and for it to gather momentum, so thought might be given to the provision of trigger materials such as a short video clip, case study or newspaper article to contextualise and give an initial focus.

Ensuring an outcome

When discussion goes well, it can be easy for learners to get caught up in the process, enjoying the activity but at its conclusion being less sure about exactly what has been learned. This is more marked when there is lots of digression and the discussion gradually loses focus. Summarising and drawing tentative conclusions at regular intervals can help keep matters on track and identify learning as it occurs. When summarising, however, there needs to be recognition of whose conclusions are being highlighted – *So what you seem to be saying is ...*; *It appears that you are suggesting that ...* Some form of final summary makes sure that learners leave the discussion with the main points fresh in their minds, but often a round where each member of the group briefly summarises what they have learned can be more productive.

Inductive and deductive approaches

Inductive and deductive approaches stem from the views of Bruner and Ausubel discussed in the previous chapter and refer to two possible routes to the learning of concepts and principles. Concepts can be considered as forms of schema which allow us to simplify and make sense of the complex world in which we live. This is achieved through grouping together objects or processes which possess the same characteristics. These groupings allow us to classify and organise our knowledge and experience of the world. Murphy (2002, p1) describes concepts as

> the mental glue that holds our world together ... we must rely on our concepts of the world to help us understand what is happening ... a kind of mental glue in that they tie our past experiences to our present interactions of the world, and because the concepts themselves are connected to our larger knowledge structures.

We form concepts then, when we group or classify anything. If I were to say the word 'dog' to you, what response would it trigger? You will probably conjure up in your mind an image of a four-legged animal which barks and wags its tail when happy and which is representative of all the dogs you have met to date. The word 'dog' is the label given to the concept which groups together all of those animals which possess 'dog-like' characteristics. At the same time, I would have a similar image in my mind. Concepts are the means by which we communicate knowledge and ideas with each other. On another day, if you meet a dog you have never seen before, you will be able to predict certain characteristics and behaviours it will possess despite having no prior knowledge of this particular animal. Concepts reduce the need for constant learning and also give us cues as to how to behave in new situations.

Concepts are fundamental to the subject you teach as well as to life, providing a way of organising subject knowledge and the means of communicating this knowledge to each other. Consider the examples below.

Subject	Some concepts
Accounting	Debit, credit, double-entry
Bricklaying	Bricks, mortar, plasticiser
Catering	Health, diet, nutrition
Chemistry	Acid, base, reaction

REFLECTIVE TASK
REFLECTIVE TASK

Concepts form the language of any subject specialism. Consider your own particular specialist subject. What are its basic concepts? At what stage do your learners encounter these?

Some concepts such as 'bricks' and 'mortar' are concrete in nature – we can identify them through our senses by seeing, hearing touching, tasting or smelling them. They are real to us. Others such as 'credit' and 'health' are abstract – they are ideas, processes, situations or events which cannot be directly experienced through the senses. Regardless of type, however, the acquisition of the relevant basic concepts is the first step in the learning of any subject.

Some concepts you will have encountered in your reading about teaching and learning will include:

motivation, memory, attention.

Suppose I now tell you that:

memory *is enhanced when* motivation *is high and* attention *is focused solely on the material to be learned.*

We now have a statement of the relationship between these concepts known as a 'principle'. A principle is a proposition or rule that operates within the subject you teach and links together the different ideas or concepts upon which the subject is based. The learning of subject principles is the next stage on from acquiring the necessary concepts.

Subject	Principle
Accounting	The sum of all *debits* should be equal to the sum of all *credits* in *double-entry* bookkeeping
Bricklaying	Adding *plasticiser* to a *mortar* mix gives greater adhesion between *bricks*
Catering	A *balanced* diet contains the six key *nutrient* groups essential for good *health* in appropriate amounts
Chemistry	In a *reaction* between an *acid* and a *base*, a salt and water are formed

A knowledge of the basic concepts and principles is therefore fundamental to the learning of all subjects. This begs the question of how they are best taught.

Suppose I wanted to teach you the concept of 'rolt'. First I would check that you didn't already know what a rolt is. Try the following multiple-choice question.

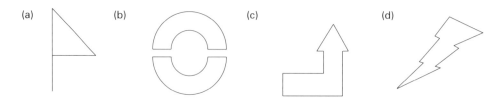

(a)　　　(b)　　　(c)　　　(d)

Which of the above is a rolt?

Assuming that you cannot answer correctly at this stage, I could now go through the following sequence:

 This is an example of a rolt

 Here is another example of a rolt

 This is not a rolt, so push it to the back of your mind

 Here is another rolt

 This is definitely not a rolt, ignore it

 This, however, is

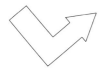 Here is a last example of a rolt

Try the test again. Which of the following is a rolt?

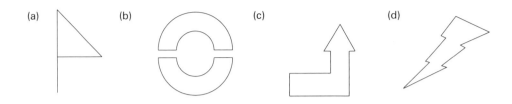

(a)   (b)   (c)   (d)

Hopefully you will now have the right answer and now recognise what a rolt is. You could probably describe it in words and arrive at a definition. Furthermore, if you now came across another rolt you had not seen before, you would recognise it for what it is.

Obviously there is no such thing as a rolt in real life but hopefully the example makes the point. A similar procedure can be adopted to teach any concept, or indeed a principle, that falls within your own subject specialism.

If you taught concepts or principles in this manner you would be using the inductive approach. The sequence adopted in the inductive approach is to start from examples and arrive at the general definition/concept or rule/principle.

Examples are presented along with some non-examples. The non-examples are used to highlight the common features or attributes in the examples and help learners to identify these for themselves. They can now use their knowledge of these common features to classify new experiences or knowledge as also being an example of this particular concept.

A similar result can be achieved by presenting positive and negative examples as pairs, as suggested by Joyce and Weil (2004, p72) who advocate the following sequence:

1. teacher presents labelled examples;
2. students compare attributes in positive and negative examples;
3. students generate and test hypotheses;
4. students state a definition according to the essential attributes.

An inductive approach follows the sequence below.

| **INDUCTIVE SEQUENCE** |
| Examples → Concept/Principle |
| Specific → General |

This is the approach favoured by Bruner, whereby learners arrive at or discover the required concepts or principles for themselves. Babies and young children who do not yet have access to language learn in this way. The inductive approach mirrors the way in which lots of learning occurs naturally. In order for this approach to work effectively in a teaching context, the choosing of appropriate examples is crucial. Examples should clearly illustrate the characteristics of the concept or principle to be learned, otherwise confusion can result.

Suppose I wanted to adopt an inductive approach to teaching the concept of 'group'. I would start by presenting and differentiating between examples and non-examples of groups.

Learners would then be asked to focus on the examples of groups and identify their common features. They would thus arrive at a list of characteristics that make a group a group. To check understanding, they would then be asked to come up with some examples of their own, giving reasons as to why they thought these also came into the category of 'group'.

Alternatively I could present an example (a number of people playing together in a band) and a non-example (a number of people in a railway carriage, travelling to the coast) and ask for a comparison between the two. This process would be repeated until the selection of common characteristics became sufficiently refined to identify a 'group'.

A different approach would be to start by defining what I meant by a 'group'.

A group is a number of people who:

- share a common goal or purpose;
- interact with each other;
- behave in line with agreed norms;
- share a common identity.

I would then illustrate my definition by reference to examples, showing how they fitted the description, and non-examples, showing how they did not fit and therefore could not be called a 'group'. This is the reverse sequence to the inductive approach. The contents are the same – examples, non-examples and general definition – but the order is different. This is the 'deductive' approach and employs the sequence shown below.

```
┌─────────────────────────────────────────┐
│           DEDUCTIVE SEQUENCE             │
│                                          │
│      Concept/Principle  →  Examples      │
│                                          │
│          General   →   Specific          │
└─────────────────────────────────────────┘
```

This is the approach favoured by Ausubel, who considers the whole picture to be the starting point in learning any new concept or principle. In practical terms it proceeds as follows.

1. The concept, principle or generalisation is first stated and then explained fully and clearly. The relationships it contains are identified and emphasised.
2. Examples are considered and in each case an explanation of how they fit and illustrate the concept or principle is explained.
3. Some non-examples are also introduced with a clear explanation as to why they do not qualify.
4. Learners are given some further examples to work through.

Each of the two approaches has its own advantages and limitations.

- Inductive is a more risky and time-consuming route but is a more active form of learning.
- Deductive can be more easily controlled but is less intrinsically motivating.

Both approaches work towards the same goal of establishing meaning and understanding, however, and which you choose is a matter of suitability and personal preference.

PRACTICAL TASK PRACTICAL TASK PRACTICAL TASK PRACTICAL TASK **PRACTICAL TASK**

Identify one area of your teaching in which you take a more deductive approach to teaching. Devise a sequence by which an inductive approach could be taken for this particular topic.

Problem-solving

Problem-solving is the process through which a solution is found when an unfamiliar situation or task is encountered. It falls within the cognitive sphere as the arrival at the solution to a problem defines the moment at which understanding occurs. It is primarily considered to be a learning activity but as you will see later, it can also provide an effective method of checking or assessing understanding. Problem-solving as a learning activity falls within the cognitive sphere as it requires and leads to understanding.

In a learning situation problem-solving can also have a considerable effect on motivation. If learners reach a successful conclusion through their own efforts, they feel a genuine sense of achievement and this has a strong positive effect on motivation. If, on the other hand, learners are unsuccessful in arriving at a solution or feel they have had to be told the solution, motivation decreases. The way in which the activity is managed largely determines which of these outcomes is achieved and this will be explored shortly, but first a consideration of the context and underlying principles of problem-solving will prove useful.

When first confronted by an unfamiliar problem, we tend to turn first to previous experience in search of a solution. We are looking to see if we have previously met a situation which is sufficiently similar to the present predicament to provide an answer. If this is the case it can be considered a form of transfer of learning – positive in this case – and the problem has been solved using what Maier (1931) termed *reproductive thinking*. If, however, the problem encountered lies outside previous experience, *productive thinking* has to be used to generate a completely new solution.

This can be achieved in two ways. An approach based on trial and error can be used where a variety of fairly random different solutions are tried, until eventually an answer is found. More in keeping with cognitive principles, however, is the adoption of a systematic approach whereby the problem solver follows a sequence of steps. Baron (2001, pp267–8) suggests that the following four steps are central to the process of problem solving:

1. problem identified and understood;
2. potential solutions generated;
3. solutions examined and evaluated;
4. solutions tried: results evaluated.

Managing problem-solving initially involves the creation of a climate of exploration and discovery in which the making of mistakes is considered a natural and acceptable part of the process. Once the fear of making mistakes has been dispelled, management takes the form of supporting learners in their problem-solving efforts, removing any barriers that may prevent them from arriving at a solution. It is important, particularly for motivation, that learners generate their own solutions. As Gagne (1985, p191) points out, *Guidance may vary in amount or completeness, always stopping short of describing the solution.*

The steps in solving problems provide a useful structure for managing problem-solving in a non-directive manner, pointing towards a number of interventions that can be usefully made. The following problems will be used to demonstrate this.

Problem 1

Can you join the nine dots in the arrangement below, by drawing four continuous straight lines and without lifting the pencil from the paper?

Problem 2

Assemble six matches in such a way that they form four congruent triangles each side of which is equal to one match length.

Problem 3

Given a balance and ten billiard balls, one of which is different in weight to the others, find out which ball is different and whether it is heavier or lighter than the others.

Stage1. Problem identified and understood

The first requirement is a problem to be solved. This is not quite as straightforward as it may seem, however, as the problem chosen makes an important contribution to the overall success of the activity. In arriving at a decision, there are two criteria to be considered.

Relevance and interest

Engaging in an activity purely for the sake of it rarely leads to a successful outcome in terms of either learning or motivation. If learners are to be fully engaged and participate enthusiastically, they must see some point in doing so. The chosen problem needs to be seen as relating directly to what is being learned and as serving a purpose as part of that learning. The manner in which the problem is presented is also important in this respect and Bruner suggests that this should be achieved in a manner designed to arouse interest and curiosity.

Challenging but achievable

To maintain motivation, learners engaging in a problem-solving activity should enter into it with a reasonable expectation of success. This is not to say that the problem presented should be easy. If too easy, there will be no real feeling of achievement in arriving at the answer and it is possible that the exercise could be perceived by learners as rather patronising. The problem has to present a challenge; learners need to feel they have metaphorically 'climbed the mountain' in order to achieve the solution. Having said that, it would be foolish to ask a group of novice climbers to tackle Everest, so achievability is just as important as challenge. A good problem attains an appropriate balance between the two and it should be evident that to arrive at this point, a sound knowledge of the learners and their capabilities is required.

Having identified a suitable problem, it now needs to be presented to learners and this can be organised in a number of different ways. Learners can work individually on problems, in pairs or in small groups, on complete problems or parts of problems. These different options give scope for a differentiated approach. When learners have been organised and the purpose and structure of the activity have been explained, the actual problem can be presented. Spoken or written instructions can be used for this purpose but whichever is considered to be the more appropriate, the problem should be stated in a clear and unambiguous manner.

Learners can now begin to work on the problem. The best strategy for the teacher at this stage is to allow them to get on with it, monitoring progress and only stepping in when it is apparent either from body language or from what is being said that it is appropriate to do so. As the activity progresses, a number of interventions should be made at appropriate stages of the problem-solving process. These are made in a systematic manner with the purpose of removing obstacles that learners may be encountering. Learners need a little time to familiarise themselves with the problem, however, before you make that first deliberate intervention. This takes the form of an enquiry as to progress but its real purpose is to ensure that everyone understands and has interpreted the problem correctly. Learners are asked to make a statement as to what they think the problem actually is. This can be checked and questioned if necessary.

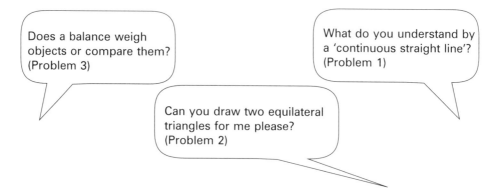

Does a balance weigh objects or compare them? (Problem 3)

What do you understand by a 'continuous straight line'? (Problem 1)

Can you draw two equilateral triangles for me please? (Problem 2)

Prior to tests or exams, learners are often told to make sure that they 'read the question properly'. To gain credit they need to answer the questions that are written on the test paper rather than the question they think is there or would like to be there. In the same way, you don't want learners wasting time and energy, leading to possible frustration, because they are tackling a problem other than the one they should be. Before moving on then, you need to be sure that everyone has an accurate perception of the problem.

Stage 2. Potential solutions generated

Learners can now be given time to start to consider potential solutions. This is not as straightforward as it might seem, however, and Snowman and Biehler (2005, p308) suggest an additional stage of *compiling relevant information* needs to be completed prior to generating solutions to problems. Problems are solved by the use of concepts and principles. Learners possess a store of these and may need help in picking out which particular concepts or principles are appropriate to this particular problem. An appropriate question to ask at this stage then, is *What kind of information are you thinking of/do you think you will need in solving this problem?*, with appropriate further discussion or questioning as required. This is the second major intervention. It can be prefaced by *Just remind me of the problem* as its function is to ensure that learners are still focused on the correct problem and are considering the appropriate factors required to arrive at a solution.

Obstacles that can exist at this stage are those of mental set and functional fixedness. Mental set is often compared with being stuck in a rut and refers to the tendency to persevere with a particular strategy which has proved successful in the past although it is either inappropriate in solving this particular problem or a better option exists. Mental set can prove useful in that it can lead to efficiency in problem-solving as it prevents the need to 'reinvent the wheel' each time we are faced with a problem. It can be considered an example of reproductive thought in that context. Mental set is not helpful, however, when a new type of problem is encountered which requires productive thinking. Functional fixedness is a specific case of mental set in which we are blinded to the possibilities of certain objects in a problem-solving situation as we consider them to have one function only. Duncker demonstrated this phenomenon in 1945 in an experiment in which participants were given a candle and a box of drawing pins. The problem was to attach the candle to the wall in an upright position so that it would burn properly. The simplest solution was to pin the empty drawing-pin box to the wall and place the candle inside it. Hardly anyone came up with this solution as they perceived the drawing pin box as exactly that – a box to hold the drawing pins.

The purpose of the third intervention is to deal with such obstacles to progress. A couple of summary questions (*What was the problem again?*, *What information did we agree you needed?*) allow a lead into *What kind of thoughts have you had so far?* and general discussion around the answers to this question should identify obstacles. The appropriate questions can then be asked to dispel these.

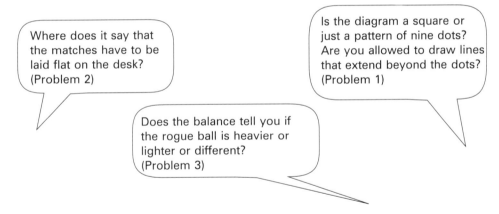

Learners should now be in a position to start thinking constructively about possible solutions to the problem.

Stage 3. Solutions examined and evaluated

The fourth intervention involves discussion, evaluation and learning from the possible solutions that learners have come up with. If no solutions are forthcoming, suggestions can be made of a 'what if' nature or analogies can be used to make the problem more accessible. Perhaps trying to work backwards from the required result rather than starting from the problem itself may prove productive as a strategy. If the previous stages have been successfully negotiated, however, learners should be able to arrive at some tentative solutions.

It is at this stage that the climate in which discussion is conducted becomes the most influential factor. It needs to be made clear, either explicitly or implicitly, that mistakes are not only acceptable but provide opportunities to refine or rethink the solutions under consideration. As with previous stages, it is important here to guide thinking through questioning rather than directly telling.

Stage 4. Solutions tried: results evaluated

Learners should complete this final stage by themselves and the role of the teacher is to confirm success by asking for the solution and its underlying rationale. A final word of praise does not go amiss here. A useful ending to the activity is to encourage some reflection, while learners are still flushed with success, on the process they have been through. What has been learned in solving this problem? Can systematic steps which apply to the solving of any problem be identified? The answers to questions like these can help learners to become more effective problem-solvers and develop a valuable life skill.

REFLECTIVE TASK

If you use problem-solving as a learning activity, reflect on the way in which you conducted it.

Did learners really arrive at their own solutions?

How much assistance did you have to offer?

Did learners find it a useful and rewarding experience or one in which frustrated them?

Did you use any of the steps and strategies outlined above to good effect in managing the activity?

Mind maps

A mind map takes the form of a diagram and is used to show or arrive at the structure of the topic under consideration. It groups together ideas around central themes and visually it represents the whole picture, illustrating the relationships between the themes contained within it. Although originally proposed by Tony Buzan (1991) as a memory aid and a way of structuring notes, the technique can be used to introduce, explain or develop a topic, and fits particularly well with Ausubel's notion of reception learning, where the starting point is an explanation of the structure of the topic. A simple mind map can be used to introduce a session and can be referred to at different stages to keep the structure of the session and its topic fresh in the mind of learners. Alternatively, it can be built up as the session progresses and new facts and ideas are encountered. Learners can work in small groups to construct their own mind maps or parts of a mind map as a short starter activity at the beginning of a session. Mind maps can also be constructed or completed at the conclusion of a session as an informal assessment method. There are a number of ways of using these but in each case, knowledge or information is being presented or constructed in a manner which demonstrates relationships and facilitates understanding and subsequently memory.

To construct a mind map, the starting point is to write down the main topic heading in the middle of the page. This is then broken down into smaller related areas which radiate from the centre of the diagram. Further thoughts and ideas are added as branches until the page is filled with a structured visual representation of the topic showing the different parts to it and the connections between these. Generally the technique works best when:

● thoughts are initially recorded in an uncritical fashion;
● the page is used as 'landscape' to allow more space for mapping;

- unlined paper is used, as lined paper tends to encourage linear thinking;
- printing (lower case) is used rather than script as it is more easily read and encourages brevity in recording ideas;
- colour is used to illustrate themes and highlight important points;
- pictures, icons or other visual cues are included as these help memory;
- arrows and lines are used to show connections.

Assessment of learning

REFLECTIVE TASK

Before you read this section on assessment, list the assessment activities that you use in your own daily practice. From the list, pick out those which you think are suitable for assessing cognitive learning and decide why you think this is the case.

Odd one out

Answer the following question:

Which of the following is the odd one out?

(a) schema
(b) insight
(c) conditioning
(d) concept.

Naturally, you will have picked (c) as your answer, but how did you arrive at that conclusion? You looked at the four different options and grouped (a), (b) and (d) together as they shared a common characteristic (they are all terms associated with a cognitive perspective on learning) which (c) did not possess. The question tested your ability to form a concept, an essential process in a cognitive perspective on learning. Another approach to assessment would be to set a comprehension passage and ask questions designed to test an understanding of the concepts contained in the passage.

These two approaches illustrate the underlying principle of the assessment of cognitive learning. It is not concerned with factual recall but with the ability to interpret and structure information and to engage in reasoned thought, and this purpose will be reflected in the assessment methods used. Cottrell (2005, pp18–31) provides a number of short activities for assessing thinking skills which can be adapted for assessment purposes. She categorises these under the headings of:

- comparison;
- sequence;
- categorising;
- following directions;
- recognising similarities.

Problem-solving

Problem: A person borrows £1000 from their bank and has to repay the loan at an interest rate of 4% per annum. What is the total amount of interest they will have to pay if the term of the loan is 5 years?

Answer: Interest = capital × rate × time
$$= 1000 \times 4 \times 5$$
$$= £20,000$$

What does the answer tell us? It is unlikely that this person understands the concept of interest if they accept that the borrower will pay back an amount 20 times the initial sum borrowed. We can also see that the concept of 'percentage' is incorrectly understood and applied. Problem-solving can tell us if principles have been merely memorised or if they have been understood. The specific mistakes also identify concepts that are improperly understood or completely misunderstood.

Essay

The essay, and similar activities such as integrated assignments, provide an open-ended form of assessment in which learners are given a certain amount of freedom to develop their own ideas and arguments. This makes it an appropriate form of assessment when the learning under examination is based around understanding and the ability to identify relationships and express these in reasoned argument.

The table below (Woolfolk, Hughes and Walkup, 2008, p671), illustrates this by listing different essay titles and showing what each is designed to assess.

Attribute to be tested	Example of essay title
Understanding cause and effect	Give three reasons why more cars are sold in Britain than in Iceland
Summarising	Summarise the story of Beowulf in 100 words or less
Decision-making	Should the death penalty be restored for terrorist murders? Defend your answer
Application of rules or principles	Where would you weigh more, on the Moon or on Mars? Explain your answer
Analysis	Why is there so much violence on football terraces?
Giving examples or illustrating principles	Name three examples of the use of the lever in your home
Making comparisons	Compare trawling and drifting as methods of catching fish
Explanation	Macbeth says *Life's but a walking shadow, a poor player that struts and frets his hour upon the stage.* Explain the meaning of this statement

The essay, however, is a method which encounters problems in the two most important characteristics of any assessment method – reliability and validity.

Reliability or consistency in the results of an assessment, when applied to the essay, has been the subject of a number of studies, all of which found wide discrepancies in the marks awarded to the same piece of work. Considering the subjective nature of the type of learning being assessed, there is a certain inevitability in this outcome, but this does little to increase confidence in the essay as an assessment method. Reliability of results can be improved by making the essay title less open and more explicit, while still allowing the writer some freedom, and by the introduction of a mark scheme which sets out the criteria by which marks should be awarded. While reliability may be less of an issue where the purpose of the assessment is formative rather than summative, it will always remain a problem to a greater or lesser degree when using the essay as an assessment method.

Validity also raises issues. The essay has its limitations relating to the sampling of course content as a whole, for instance (content validity), as it looks for in-depth treatment of selected areas rather than a more surface treatment over a greater range. Construct validity, or the degree to which a test measures what it intends to measure, can also be low as the method tends to favour those with good writing skills. It is possible that learners possess a sound understanding of the subject but do not gain credit for this understanding due to an inability to adequately express themselves in a written form.

The essay then, provides an appropriate method of assessing understanding and thinking skills but careful thought needs to be given to the setting of the essay title so that it is phrased in a manner that makes it evident to the learner exactly what is required of them, and suitable strategies such as mark schemes and double marking need to be adopted to increase the reliability of the results obtained.

Classroom management

By now you should be familiar with the idea that cognitivists are interested in the whole picture and how the different parts contained within it relate to each other. They do not view anything in isolation.

This principle also holds true for classroom management. Unlike behaviourism where the behaviour itself is the sole concern, behaviour is viewed as merely one part of a more complex picture in a cognitive approach, and in order to arrive at an understanding of behaviour, the person as a whole has to be taken into consideration.

McPhillimy (1996, p57) reminds us that *another central aspect of the cognitive approach is the importance it attaches to the influence on a pupil's behaviour of his self-concept*. Self-concept is dealt with in more detail in Chapter 6, where it is described as *everyone has their own particular view of themselves and their situation*. For the purpose of this discussion, however, there are two important facts concerning self-concept.

1. It is situational – it takes on a different form in different situations. The way a person views themselves in a social situation may be different from the way they view themselves in a learning situation, which may in turn be different from the way they view themselves in a sporting situation, for example.
2. It can either be positive – people have an optimistic, upbeat picture of themselves – or negative – the picture is pessimistic and gloomy.

As we are considering self-concept in an educational setting, the particular form of self-concept that is of interest is what is known as the academic self-concept, the way in which people view themselves in a learning situation.

A positive academic self-concept will result from consistent previous success in learning. Learning is not something to be feared and the learner with a positive self-concept will approach whatever learning tasks are set with an expectation of success. This results in a genuine effort and a positive attitude to learning and so inappropriate behaviour is unlikely.

Unfortunately, learners do not all possess a positive academic self-concept. The lifelong learning sector is often seen as a second chance and in further education in particular, a proportion of learners will bring a negative academic self-concept to the learning situation. Expectations are now of difficulty and failure and are accompanied by feelings of anxiety and unhappiness. Learners who come into the learning environment with such a frame of mind and find their worst fears confirmed, may simply not try, since, if you don't try to be successful, you cannot fail. How is this perceived by teachers?

> *No one likes failure and difficulty (how many adults persist with a sport or leisure activity for which they have little talent?), but teachers who have all been relatively successful academically, often find it difficult to appreciate just how dispiriting it is for pupils to have to persist day in and day out in activities where they feel doomed to failure. 'Not trying' is therefore often a means to avoid failing, rather than defiance of the teacher's wishes.*

> (McPhillimy, 1996, p59)

Other tactics employed by learners in the evading of failure include avoidance strategies such as not bringing equipment, self deprecation – *I've never been any good at...*, putting the blame elsewhere – on the teacher, the boring nature of the subject, and as a last resort a refusal to do the work.

The remedy here is self-evident, although not always straightforward to apply in practice, and lies in trying to turn a negative self-concept into one of a positive nature. Establishing some kind of rapport or relationship with learners can have a positive effect on self-concept in general but learners need to experience success in their learning to turn around a negative academic self-concept. This can be achieved by setting short-term achievable targets accompanied by work which is carefully structured to ensure a successful outcome. It is not only success itself that is important, however, but the learner's recognition and acceptance of that success as their own and this is the main function of the target-based approach.

A cognitive approach does not see behaviour as the main issue but rather as a symptom of a deeper underlying problem. It is very different from a behaviourist approach in that it demands a different relationship between teacher and learner and its strategies are of a more general nature than those of behaviourism, which targets the specific behaviour.

A SUMMARY OF **KEY POINTS**

> Planning, in the cognitive approach, centres on the big picture and can start from a consideration of activities or 'educational encounters' rather than the expected learning outcome.

> The cognitive perspective underpins the process approach to curriculum in which the outcome is considered to be of less importance than the process of learning that is undertaken.

> The purpose of teaching methods in a cognitive approach is to promote understanding and reasoned thinking. Discussion, in which all learners participate in the same activity but arrive at their own individual conclusions, is an example of this approach.

> Ausubel suggests that the most effective sequence in teaching is to start from a generalisation and use examples as illustrations to deepen understanding. This is known as the deductive approach.

> Bruner advocates the inductive approach in which learners arrive at the generalistion themselves through a process of discovery. This is achieved through drawing out general characteristics from a series of examples and non-examples of the generalisation.

> Problem-solving is an activity which can be used as both a learning activity and an assessment method. When used as a teaching method, the role of the teacher is to ease learners through the problem-solving process with a series of interventions that ensure learners arrive at the correct answer through their own endeavours.

> Mind maps illustrate the structure of a topic under consideration and show the relationships between its different facets or parts. They can be used in a number of ways by either teachers or learners to structure learning.

> Assessment methods in a cognitive approach are designed to test for understanding, whether learners can identify relationships and present reasoned arguments.

> The essay is the main assessment method used in a cognitive approach to learning. While it presents some problems relating to reliability and validity of results, it allows learners to demonstrate under-standing and original thinking.

> Classroom management techniques are not directed at inappropriate behaviours but regard these as a symptom of a greater problem. The strategies used are intended to convert the learner's self-concept from a negative to a positive state, thus leading to appropriate forms of behaviour.

REFERENCES REFERENCES **REFERENCES** REFERENCES REFERENCES REFERENCES

Ausubel, D (1963) *The psychology of meaningful verbal learning*. New York: Grune and Stratton.

Baron, RA (2001) *Psychology* (5th edn). Boston, London: Allyn and Bacon.

Bruner, J (1963) *The process of education.* Cambridge, MA: Harvard University Press.

Buzan, T (1991) *The mind map book*. New York: Penguin.

Cottrell, S (2005) *Critical thinking skills.* Basingstoke, New York: Palgrave Macmillan.

Eisner, E (1969) Instructional and expressive educational objectives: their formulation and use In curriculum, in WJ Popham, et al. *American Educational Research Association Monograph Series on Curriculum Evaluation* p3–18. Washington DC: American Educational Research Association.

Gagne, RM (1985) *The conditions of learning and theory of instruction* (4th edn). New York: Holt Rinehart and Winston.

Joyce, B and Weil, M (2004) *Models of teaching* (7th edn). New Jersey: Prentice-Hall.

Maier, NRF (1931) Reasoning in humans: The solution of a problem and its appearance in consciousness. *Journal of Comparative Psychology*, 13: 181–94.

McPhillimy, B (1996) *Controlling your class.* Chichester: John Wiley & Sons.

Murphy, G (2002) *The big book of concepts*. Cambridge, MA: MIT Press.

Stenhouse, L (1975) *An introduction to curriculum research and development*. Heinemann Educational.

Snowman, J and Biehler, R (2005) *Psychology applied to teaching* (11th edn). Boston, New York: Houghton Mifflin.

Woolfolk, A, Hughes, M and Walkup, V (2008) *Psychology in education*. Harlow, Essex: Pearson Education.

6
The humanistic approach

Chapter overview and objectives

Behaviourism focuses on behaviour itself; cognitivism concerns itself with meaning and under-standing. In this chapter the emphasis shifts again, this time towards a consideration of learners and the processes they go through in learning. Lying at the heart of the humanistic perspective on learning is the person. The purpose of this chapter is not to define learning and identify its characteristics but rather to explore the relationship between learning and learners.

When you have worked through this chapter you will be able to:

- **identify the characteristics of a humanistic perspective;**
- **describe Maslow's hierarchy of needs and the importance of self-actualisation;**
- **identify the background to the work of Carl Rogers and relate this to an educational context;**
- **recognise the importance of the teacher–learner relationship in a humanistic approach and identify ways of establishing such a relationship;**
- **determine the relationship between the humanistic perspective and a student-centred approach to learning;**
- **evaluate the assumptions upon which such an approach is based;**
- **differentiate between teaching and facilitation;**
- **describe Heron's dimensions and modes of facilitation;**
- **relate humanistic principles to the activities of Summerhill school.**

This chapter contributes to the following values and areas of professional knowledge as contained in the LLUK professional standards for teachers, tutors and trainers in the lifelong learning sector:

AS4, BS2, CS4, DS3

AK1.1, AK4.1, AK4.3, BK1.1, BK1.2, BK1.3, BK2.1, BK2.7, CK3.1

Humanism as the 'third force'

The dominant perspectives in psychology in the 1940s and 1950s were behaviourism and the psychoanalytic approach proposed by Freud. As has been seen, behaviourism regarded humans as mechanistic beings whose behaviours are controlled by external factors such as reward and punishment. The external environment to which they respond determines how they behave. Behaviourism, with its insistence on the importance of the external environment, denies the existence of free will. It suggests that behaviour is predictable and takes no account of the ability to make choices that establish actions. The psychoanalytic approach, on the other hand, suggested that humans are instinctive, irrational beings whose behaviour is influenced by the workings of the unconscious mind which contains forgotten or repressed memories and experiences. Psychoanalytic approaches also suggest that people's actions and behaviours are controlled by factors other than free will. Increasingly these two perspectives were seen as presenting a limiting view of humanity and in the early

1960s, a group of psychologists which included Abraham Maslow and Carl Rogers began to ask themselves what it is that makes humans 'human'. The conclusions they arrived at formed the basis of an alternative to these two main theories and they called it 'third force' psychology, or humanistic psychology.

Humanist thinkers felt that both the psychoanalytic approach and behaviorism took an overly pessimistic view of the human condition. Freud formulated his ideas through his work with patients suffering from a range of neurotic disorders, leading Maslow (1954, p236) to comment (in language we would now consider to be politically incorrect) that:

> the study of crippled, stunted, immature, and unhealthy specimens can yield only a cripple psychology and a cripple philosophy.

He later elaborates on this statement, saying:

> When you select out for careful study very fine and healthy people, strong people, creative people, saintly people, sagacious people...then you get a very different view of mankind. You are asking how tall can people grow, what can a human being become?

(Maslow, 1971, p43)

Maslow, in arriving at his 'hierarchy of needs', studied and interviewed people he regarded as being highly successful in their chosen field. The humanistic perspective stresses everything that is positive and hopeful about humans. It recognises the individuality of the person and their ability to take control of their own destiny.

The underlying principles of the humanistic approach are:

- it is an optimistic view of humanity in which individuals strive, within their own personal limitations, to achieve the maximum personal growth;
- it is focused on the person but stresses individuality or uniqueness of the person rather than the similarities in people;
- it views people as being self-determining, free to make their own choices;
- it considers that psychology should concern itself with the experience of the individual as seen through their own eyes (phenomenology);
- that distant, objective scientific methods are therefore inappropriate in studying human beings.

The major aim of the humanistic approach is:

- to help people to maximise their potential for personal growth.

Abraham Maslow

Maslow is best known for his hierachy of needs, a study of motivation which is normally represented in the form of a triangle as below:

Maslow believed in the existence of two different categories of need or motivational state. The first of these categories included, in ascending order:

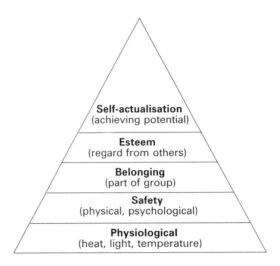

1. **Physiological**   air, drink, food, sleep, shelter, warmth, sex
2. **Safety/security**   protection from danger, security, stability
3. **Belongingness and love**   acceptance by others, family, relationships
4. **Esteem**   achievement, respect, approval, recognition

Maslow called the four levels in this first category 'deficiency needs' (D-motives), as a lack of satisfaction in these results in a deficiency of some kind that motivates people to act. Deficiency needs are fulfilled in a hierarchical order, as only unsatisfied needs are motivators. Once a need is satisfied, the next highest level becomes the motivator.

The second category of needs, Maslow called 'growth needs' or 'being-needs' (B-motives). Behaviour in this case is motivated not by deficiencies but by the desire for personal growth. Growth needs become the major motivating force only when the deficiency needs have been met. In his original model, Maslow identified only one level of growth need:

5. **Self-actualisation** self-fulfilment, realising personal potential, seeking personal growth

In later versions of the model, self-actualisation is sub-divided into a number of other levels, which expanded on the nature and meaning of self actualisation itself. The final set of growth levels consists of:

5. **Cognitive**   knowledge, meaning, etc.
6. **Aesthetic**   appreciation and search for beauty, balance, form, etc.
7. **Self-Actualisation**   self-fulfilment, realising personal potential, seeking personal growth
8. **Transcendence**   helping others to achieve self-actualisation.

Deficiency needs are considered as basic, and once fulfilled, they stop being motivators. As the song says *you don't miss your water till your well runs dry*. With growth needs, on the other hand, the motivation for psychological growth and development cannot be so easily satisfied. Fulfilment of growth needs serves to increase motivation, and further activity results. Growth needs are therefore a form of intrinsic motivation. Maslow considered this to be a different type of intrinsic motivation, however, from that encountered in cognitive psychology. Cognitivists consider intrinsic motivation to be based on reduction of tension – the discomfort felt when meaning is not evident, for instance. To Maslow, intrinsic motivation as typified by growth needs is a rewarding and exciting process which increases and grows further rather than decreasing and disappearing when it has met its purpose.

> *Growth is, in itself, a rewarding and exciting process . . . like playing the violin or being a good carpenter . . . It is simply inaccurate to speak in such instances of tension-reduction, implying therefore getting rid of an annoying state. For these states are not annoying.*

(Maslow, 1968, pp29–31)

It is not essential for all needs to be met, as people can and do live in various states of contentedness, but from a humanist perspective, the drive towards self-actualisation is considered to be the ideal to work towards achieving.

Carl Rogers

Rogers started his career as a clinical psychologist and it is from this context that his early work was derived. The prevailing approach at the time was what is now termed directive. In his book *On becoming a person*, Rogers (1989, p32) describes how he used to ask himself how he could treat, cure or change people. His question later changed to asking himself how he could provide a relationship which the client might use for their own personal growth. His answer provided the basis for his non-directive, or client-centred, approach to psychotherapy.

Rogers' theory grew out of his experiences as a clinical psychologist. He regarded experience as *the highest authority* (1989, p23), and it led him to form a number of beliefs about human nature. First and foremost, he believed that people are innately good and even when dealing with the most extreme cases in therapy *it has been my experience that persons have a basically positive direction* (1989, p26) and it is this belief which is basic to the whole approach. Like Maslow, Rogers believed that all people possess a self-actualising tendency which causes them to pursue personal development as a goal in life and develop into mature and healthy beings. His own work as a clinical psychologist demonstrated all too clearly, however, that this was not always the case. What then would prevent personal development and growth?

Central to Rogers' theory is the notion of the human organism and 'the capacity of the human individual for developing her own potentiality' (Kirschenbaum and Landhenderson, 1989, p313). He saw conditional and unconditional positive regard (1989, p283) as key in the development of the self concept. Unconditional positive regard opens up the opportunity of self actualisation but those raised in a climate of conditional positive regard feel a need to match external conditions (described by Rogers as *conditions of worth*) that have been laid down by others.

Self-concept is generally regarded as comprising three components:

1. self-image – how the person sees themselves;
2. self-esteem – how much value the person places upon themselves;
3. ideal self – how the person should or would like to be.

If the human organism and ideal self are in a state of balance, the result is a well-adjusted individual. If there is an imbalance or mismatch between them, a state of incongruity exists and psychological problems will arise. Therapeutic measures involve the identification and resolution of such an imbalance. The question now arises as to who is best placed to do this. Humanism stresses the uniqueness of the person and favours a phenomenological approach. Against this background, Rogers (1989, p12) was of the opinion that:

> it is the client who knows what hurts, what directions to go, what problems are crucial, what experiences have been deeply buried. It began to occur to me that unless I had a need to demonstrate my own cleverness and learning, I would do better to rely on the client for the direction of movement in the process.

Implicit in this statement is a belief that clients have the capability to solve their own problems. In life this appeared not to be the case, however, and it now became the role of the therapist to provide an environment in which the client could reflect upon their situation, clarify their thoughts and thus gain sufficient insight to eventually arrive at a satisfactory conclusion. The therapist's role has changed from one of authority or expertise, advising or providing solutions, to one of facilitating the process of clients arriving at their own solutions, and the term 'facilitator' was adopted to acknowledge this change.

What then, does the facilitator have to do? Rogers identified three characteristics, which he deemed as 'necessary and sufficient', that the facilitator needs to possess:

- **congruence**   genuineness, honesty with the client and self;
- **empathy**   the ability to feel what the client feels – to see the client's emotional perspective;
- **respect**   acceptance, unconditional positive regard towards the client.

The facilitator creates a warm and supporting environment and communicates this to the client, thus creating the conditions that correspond with Rogers' famous quote *I know I cannot teach anyone anything, I can only provide an environment in which he can learn.*

The key factor in the Rogerian approach is a shift in control of the whole process away from the therapist and towards the client. There is a move away from dependency towards independence as he considers that it is only in this manner that true learning can occur. To clarify his position he uses the analogy of riding a bike. He suggests that when you help a child to learn to ride a bike, you can't just tell them how. They have to try it for themselves. And you can't hold them up the whole time either. There comes a point when you have to let them go. If they fall, they fall, but if you hang on, they never learn.

REFLECTIVE TASK

The next section explores the concept of student-centredness. Before you read it, write down what you consider to be the most student-centred aspect of your current teaching. Now write down what you consider to be the least student-centred aspect of your teaching. From a comparison of the two examples, come up with a definition of what you consider student-centred to mean.

Rogers considered that his ideas and approaches could work equally well in an educational context and set out his thoughts in *Freedom to learn* in 1969, subtitled *what education might be*. In this, Rogers considered and critiqued what was then current practice before suggesting an alternative approach based on his experiences in introducing the client-centred approach. In the educational setting, the term 'student-centred' was substituted for client-centred. In this approach learners take on responsibility for their own learning and the teacher adopts the role of facilitator, becoming a resource for learners rather than a director of their learning. The relationship between teacher and learner assumes greater significance, as does the importance of setting an environment which is most conducive to learning.

Rogers' writing tends to focus on the learner and the attitudes of the teacher which will encourage learning rather than identifying specific methods or techniques of instruction.

Brandes and Ginnis (1986) suggest a number of strategies appropriate to a student-centred approach, including:

- the circle;
- the round;
- brainstorming;
- games;
- open discussion;
- problem-solving;
- contracts.

Jennifer Rogers (2007, p107) adds discussion, role play and simulation to the list.

There is agreement, however, that what is important is not so much the activities engaged in, but rather the climate and relationships which are formed. Brandes and Ginnis (1986, p6) state that *in essence, student-centred learning is not a bag of tricks; it is about attitudes and relationships* and they define student-centredness as *a system of providing learning which has the student at its heart* (1986, p1). It can be seen that the determining factor in establishing a student-centred approach is the relationship which exists between learner and teacher. This relationship then determines the role of the teacher and the types of activities which might be employed.

It has been argued that the humanistic approach is more philosophical than psychological as it is based around a number of assumptions stated by Rogers. These assumptions arose from his interpretation of an amalgam of his own experience and the experience of others rather than from any form of scientific-based enquiry. An adaptation of these assumptions, taken from *Freedom to learn* (1969, pp157–64) is listed below.

- Learning is a natural human drive; everyone has a natural potentiality for learning.
- A person only learns what he or she perceives to be necessary for the maintenance or enhancement of his/her own self.
- Learning is maximised in a threat-free atmosphere.
- Learning is acquired through experience.
- Learning is facilitated when the learner participates responsibly in the learning process. When the learner chooses the goals, helps to discover learning resources, formulates problems, decides courses of action, lives with the consequences of each of these choices, then significant learning occurs.
- Learning involving the whole learner, feelings as well as intellect, is the most lasting and pervasive kind of learning.
- Independence, creativity and self-reliance are all facilitated when self-criticism is encouraged and self-evaluation is seen to be more important than evaluation by others.
- The most useful learning is learning about the process of learning.

PRACTICAL TASK **PRACTICAL TASK** **PRACTICAL TASK**

Work through the assumptions above. For each one, start off by stating whether you agree, disagree or are undecided. Now go back and write down one reason for each of your responses.

The above assumptions underpin a student-centred approach and it is evident that the approach cannot be employed in any meaningful way by anyone who does not whole-heartedly agree with them.

To give some context to each statement, some of Rogers' thoughts on each assumption are listed below. As you read through each, reflect on your own thoughts as expressed in your answers to the practical task above.

1. Everyone is born with a natural curiosity about their world. This is not always obvious as learning of any real significance can be painful, either physically (falling off a bicycle when learning to ride) or psychologically (learning you are not quite as clever as you thought). Nonetheless, the natural desire to learn is the stronger force in almost all instances and can be relied upon to drive learning forward. This natural desire to learn is released under suitable conditions. The educational system within which we work tends to be restrictive and frequently blunts this natural curiosity.
2. Rogers quotes the example of two students taking a course in statistics; one because he needs it to complete a research project, the other because there is a gap in his timetable that must be filled. Learners need to see the reason or purpose behind their learning in order to fully engage in it.
3. Threats can take either a physical or psychological form. Rogers does not say that learning does not take place under threatening conditions but that it tends to be resisted and is much more likely to occur when the level of threat is low. A poor reader who is made to read aloud in public will make less progress for instance, than one who experiences a supportive, understanding environment. Rogers distinguishes between threats which can result in significant learning – we learn very quickly not to touch hot objects – and threats to the perception of self, such as humiliation, ridicule, sarcasm, which interfere strongly with learning.
4. Rogers believes that *direct experiential confrontation with practical problems, social problems, ethical and philosophical problems, personal issues and research problems, is one of the most effective modes of promoting learning*.
5. Participative learning, especially when learners have some control over the process, is far more effective than passive learning. Note that living with the consequences of these choices is an important part of this process.
6. Learning does not take place only from the neck up and Rogers cites the examples of painting, poetry, sculpture which involve the whole person as particularly good illustrations of this.
7. Dependence and independence in learning lie at the heart of this principle. An over-reliance on the judgments of others leads to dependence and learners should be given every opportunity to self-assess and self-evaluate in order to become self-reliant and independent in their learning.
8. The rate of change is such that knowledge becomes outdated very quickly. Rogers suggests that the survival of current cultures depends upon developing individuals who are not reliant on *a static kind of learning of information* but for whom change is the norm. The skills relating to learning are thus more useful than the accumulation of knowledge.

You will doubtless agree with some of Rogers' assumptions and disagree with others. What is perhaps most important is that you now recognise what your own assumptions are. Assume for a moment that you agree in all respects with what Rogers has to say. How would you go about teaching? What activities would you engage in? Write down your own thoughts before comparing them with what Rogers considers to be a natural consequence of believing what he believes.

The following is an adaptation of the guidelines for facilitation that Rogers presents in *Freedom to learn*, pp164–6.

In teaching or, as Roger prefers, facilitation of learning, the teacher, or facilitator:

- sets a climate for learning, characterised by openness and trust;
- helps to elicit and clarify the learner's own purposes and motivation for learning as well as the more general purpose of the group;
- relies, with the majority, on the individual's own drives and purposes as the motivation for learning;
- organises and provides the widest possible range of resources for learning;
- acts as a flexible resource to be used by learners;
- accepts learners expressing their feelings as well as their thoughts;
- participates as a fellow learner and expresses feelings and ideas as a member of the learning group;
- is alert to learners' emotions and to interpersonal tensions, and is prepared to bring these into the open;
- recognises and accepts his/her own limitations.

REFLECTIVE TASK

Did you agree with what Rogers suggests? How much of the above do you, can you or would you like to incorporate into your own practice?

Summerhill School

One of the first attempts to translate humanistic principles into some kind of practice took place at Summerhill School in Suffolk. The school was founded by A. S. Neill in 1921 and still operates to this day very much on humanistic principles. Neill strongly believed in the personal freedom of children, stating that

> *a child is innately wise and realistic. If left to himself without adult suggestion of any kind he will develop as far as he is capable of developing.*
>
> (Neill, 1960, p4)

This was reflected in the day-to-day running of his school. Perhaps one of the more contentious practices was optional attendance at lessons, based on the belief that children learn more effectively when they learn by choice rather than by compulsion. It was thought that as attendance was on a voluntary basis, the lessons themselves could be made more rigorous. As well as the normal provision there were two classrooms, the workshop and the art room, which operated on a drop-in basis and could be used by anyone, with the appropriate supervision, at any time.

Another underpinning belief was that children should progress at their own pace, rather than having to meet a set standard by a certain age. Children were therefore placed in classes not by age but according to their ability in a given subject. A class could thus contain a group of pupils of widely varying ages and currently, GCSE examinations can be taken by children as young as 13 if it is thought appropriate.

This notion of freedom is not the same as a completely permissive approach which takes no account of the rights of others. The school was, and still is, managed as a democratic community through school meetings which are held three times a week and attended by both staff and pupils, each of whom has an equal voice and vote when decisions are made. At these meetings, school rules are devised or modified, contraventions of rules are dealt with in an open forum and any issues affecting life as part of the school community are discussed.

Neill felt that if discipline was externally imposed, children were unlikely to develop self-discipline. He considered that children who attended Summerhill were likely to emerge with greater self-discipline and better-developed critical thinking skills than children who were taught in a climate of compulsion. This is not a quick process, however, and adapting to an environment of freedom is more difficult for some than others.

Neill's philosophy is not without its critics and the school even went to court after a potential closure order was issued by the government following an Ofsted inspection in 1999. At issue was the school's policy of voluntary attendance at lessons but the school's position was upheld and it has recently (2007) received a favourable Ofsted report.

Facilitation

It has become evident that one of the more significant features of a humanistic approach is the role of the teacher as facilitator. This is a term which is employed in many areas of life other than education and proves rather difficult to pin down and define. Its purpose is fairly clear as the roots of the word come from the Latin *facilis* which means 'to make something easy'. In terms of education, it would seem that the facilitator makes learning easy for others. This is generally associated with an accompanying or resulting process of empowerment whereby the others in question begin to take control and responsibility for their own learning. This section refers to the work of Rogers and John Heron in coming to an understanding of what is meant by facilitation as far as education is concerned. Before reading on, complete the reflective task below.

REFLECTIVE TASK

What does facilitation mean to you? Write down your own description or definition. It might help to contemplate examples of anyone you know and consider to be facilitative in their approach to teaching and learning. What particular qualities do they possess? What kind of things do they do?

Although within an educational context, the concept of facilitation can be traced back to writers such as Dewey, it is Rogers who is largely credited with bringing it to the forefront of thinking and practice. As has been seen, Rogers considers relationships as the most significant factor in bringing about learning:

The initiation of such learning rests not upon the teaching skills of the leader, not upon his scholarly knowledge of the field, not upon his curricular planning, not upon his use of audiovisual aids, not upon the programmed learning he utilizes, not upon his lectures and presentations, not upon an abundance of books, though each of these might at one time or another be utilized as an important resource. No, the facilitation of learning rests upon certain attitudinal qualities which exist in the personal relationship *between the facilitator and learner.*

(Rogers, 1969, p105)

Rogers consequently places great importance on the qualities that a teacher would need to possess in order to establish the kind of relationship he sees as essential to the process of facilitation. There are three of these.

1. Realness or genuineness

This simply means to be oneself. Rogers compares this with what he considers to be a customary practice of putting on a mask or façade of being the teacher and removing it only at the end of the day. His own experience suggested that the more genuine he was in the relationship, the more helpful and productive it was. Genuineness involves the teacher, or facilitator, in expressing their own feelings, whether positive or negative, as part of establishing a relationship with learners as this is a major part of being 'real'.

2. Acceptance

The second quality involves accepting learners for what they are in an uncritical, non-judgmental manner. This means a respect or even liking for learners regardless of the attitudes and behaviours they may sometimes display. It is an acceptance that all learners have a worth in their own right and are ultimately trustworthy. Rogers (1969, p109) describes it as *a prizing of the learner as an imperfect human being with many feelings, many potentialities*. Learners who experience such acceptance feel they are entering a relationship of warmth and safety and are thus much more able to respond in a more honest and open manner.

3. Understanding

The third quality is based around an empathetic understanding of learners – the ability to be able to see the world as they see it, to 'stand in their shoes'. Rogers (1969, p112) cites examples of *how deeply appreciative students feel when they are simply* understood – *not evaluated, not judged, simply understood from their* own *point of view, not the teacher's.*

Rogers sees facilitation as an expression of a relationship based on genuineness, and an acceptance and understanding of learners – not always easy to achieve and virtually impossible without the belief that there is an innate goodness that exists in everyone.

Relationships can be difficult – they are not systematic or logical. Identifying the necessary personal qualities for relationship-building and describing their effective use or existence in others is one thing. Possessing such qualities or having sufficient self-awareness to develop them is most definitely another. Rogers seems to have been a 'born facilitator', possessing an abundance of the qualities and skills he sees as important but the kind of relationship he describes may not sit comfortably with many teachers who prefer to maintain some professional distance between themselves and their learners, regarding such openness as undesirable or inappropriate. If so, they are acting upon a different set of assumptions regarding the nature of learning and learners from those that Rogers subscribes to. That is quite OK and Rogers would agree that people should act in a way that is true to themselves. The situation also provides an illustration of one of the main points that this book is trying to make and is perhaps more significant in this particular chapter than in others. There are a number of different views of learning which are identified by different theories of learning. No one view is more correct or better than another – they are simply different. The particular view of learning and learners that a person holds, however, is what determines their whole approach to the practice of teaching.

Although Rogers' three attributes are obviously important for effective facilitation, they do not give specific guidance as to what a facilitator actually does – the kind of behaviours and actions that might be expected. Looking beyond Rogers, another, although complementary view of facilitation is expressed by Hunter, Bailey and Taylor (1993, p5):

> *Facilitation is about process – how you do something – rather than the content – what you do. A facilitator is a process guide; someone who makes a process easier or more convenient to use. Facilitation is about movement – moving from A to B. The facilitator helps to guide group members towards their chosen destination. Facilitation makes it easier to get to an agreed destination.*

Facilitation then, is regarded as relating to process rather than content and the facilitator is considered to be a guide. The two important concepts here are 'process' and 'guide'. Syllabi and schemes of work identify the content of what is to be taught in a fairly unambiguous manner, but here the focus is not content but process – it is less clear what process involves and also how 'guide' might be defined in this context. John Heron (1999) has devised a facilitation styles model which provides some clarification in these areas.

Heron divides facilitation into six dimensions, which can be regarded as the different aspects of process that the facilitator is concerned with, and three modes which describe different styles of intervention or ways of guiding learners.

Considering Heron's dimensions first, these are as follows.

1. Planning – to do with the aims of the group and what it should do in order to fulfil these. Planning is deemed to involve a consideration of objectives, programme, methods, resources, assessment and evaluation.
2. Meaning – how the group makes sense of what they are doing and acquire understanding. Heron identifies four kinds of understanding – conceptual (ideas, theories), imaginal (symbols, language), practical (behaviours, skills) and experiential (direct experience).
3. Confronting – dealing with rigidity or resistance within the group which might interfere with learning. This can be caused by habit, anxiety, lack of knowledge or experience or merely a preference for taking the easiest route.
4. Feeling – the management of feelings and emotion within the group. Emotions can be positive, calling for interventions designed to raise awareness, or negative, in which case interventions will look to identify, interrupt and redirect energy into more positive directions.
5. Structuring – implementing the decisions made regarding methods. How best to carry out and structure the learning activities that the group will engage in.

6. Valuing – creating the appropriate climate in which learning is to take place. This dimension aligns itself closely with Rogers' views on relationships as Heron (1999, p297) seeks to *create a climate of respect for persons and personal autonomy, in which group members feel valued and honoured, so that they can become more authentic, disclosing their true needs and interests, finding their integrity, determining their own reality and humanity.*

Heron's dimensions help in identifying the areas into which the facilitator's energy and efforts are directed. The next consideration is the manner in which this might be achieved; here Heron suggests three alternative ways or modes of engaging in the facilitative process.

The modes of facilitation examine the different styles that can be adopted and are largely concerned with the balance of power between facilitator and group.

In the first of these, the hierarchical mode, power resides with the facilitator who directs and acts on behalf of the group, making decisions and taking on responsibility for all of the dimensions of the learning process outlined above.

If the facilitator and the group share the responsibility, they are operating in the co-operative mode. The role of the facilitator is now one of collaboration. Views are shared and the facilitator's view, although influential, is not final but contributes to an agreed or negotiated outcome.

The autonomous mode gives the group the freedom to find their own way, without inter-vention. This does not mean the facilitator takes on a purely passive role but rather works to create the conditions which allow the group to become self-directing.

In the first instance the facilitator *does it* for *the group*, in the second, *does it* with *the group*, and in the final mode *gives it* to *the group* (Heron, 1999, p338).

REFLECTIVE TASK

Consider your own teaching. Can you relate to any of Heron's dimensions of the facilitative process? Identify an example of your use of each of the styles of facilitation: hierarchical, co-operative, auton-omous. Why did you adopt each particular style on these occasions? Was it the most appropriate style to use?

Heron's intention in devising this classification was not to show that different facilitators used different styles but that different styles are possible and the good facilitator will be able to access each of these styles as appropriate. Styles may be individual to some extent, depend-ing upon the particular beliefs, values, confidence and expertise of the individual facilitator; they may depend partly on the nature of the task to be completed or the objectives to be achieved. The style the facilitator adopts, however, is largely determined by the knowledge, experience and stage of development of the group.

In the early stages of its development and lacking the necessary knowledge and skills, a group will look to the facilitator for guidance and direction and so the hierarchical mode is an appropriate style to adopt in this instance. As confidence, cohesion, knowledge and skills increase within the group, a more co-operative style becomes appropriate, the group playing a much more active part in the decision-making process. Eventually, when the group has reached an appropriate level of maturity, the facilitator will take much more of a back seat as the autonomous mode becomes the most suitable style to adopt.

Facilitation style needs to respond to the nature of the group but will also involve efforts to move groups away from dependency on the facilitator towards a more independent status. Although in the above example, the three modes of facilitation are employed in a linear or sequential manner, the reality is that the facilitator needs to be *flexible in moving from mode to mode and dimension to dimension in the light of the changing situation of the group* (Heron, 1999, p9). The styles themselves are not mutually exclusive and a combination of modes can be employed. Heron (1999, p336) identifies seven ways of combining the different modes.

What is perhaps most striking about Heron's work is that he dispels the popular belief that facilitation is characterised by a 'softly softly' approach, but can legitimately be quite directive. If a group has insufficient background to cope with even a small amount of autonomy, then 'to make something easy' for them will require a structured approach. As Candy (1987, p163) says:

> to force learners into self-directed or learner controlled mode for which they may feel unprepared, seems, to me, every bit as unethical as denying freedom when it is demanded.

Assessment of learning

When an assessment takes place, it is usual to turn to some kind of referencing system to make sense of the score achieved. If, for instance, you achieve a score of 15 in a test, what does that score of 15 mean? By itself, it is fairly meaningless.

One way in which a judgment is made is to compare the test performance with a number of set criteria. If a sufficient number of appropriate criteria are met, the test is passed; if not, the result is failure. The driving test is an example of this approach. A pass mark can be used as an indication of the criteria that are required to be fulfilled. Thus, if the pass mark for your test is 12, your score of 15 is more than acceptable, whereas with a pass mark of 20, your score is viewed very differently. This approach is known as criterion-referencing. Alternatively, the measure of your success could be comparison against the scores of everyone else who had taken the same test. If most people had scored 18, 19, 20 or the average score was 19, then 15 does not compare that well. If, however, most other people had scores in the region of 11, 12, 13 or the average score was less than 15, you would have reason to be pleased with your performance. If the scores of others are taken as the point of comparison, the approach used is known as norm-referencing.

A humanistic approach concerns itself with the uniqueness of the individual and so would not look to an externally set standard or the performance of others as a point of reference against which to measure performance. The type of referencing that is appropriate within a humanistic approach to learning is known as ipsative referencing. Ipsative referencing reflects individual achievement and so the point of comparison is the previous or usual performance of that individual. Self-actualisation is a measure of individual potential and ipsative referencing explores whether or not personal progress is being made; it is therefore developmental rather than judgmental in nature.

In an educational system which is driven by results and accountability, however, it is the reaching of a set standard (criterion-referencing), the achievement of a higher grade than others (norm-referencing) or a referencing system involving a combination of these two elements which is regarded as crucial.

This chapter has examined the humanistic approach and its application in an educational setting as student-centred learning. The demands it places on teachers have also been explored along with the qualities required to successfully meet these. With respect to your own teaching, you may have embraced this view of learning or alternatively decided it is inappropriate or cannot work for you. To employ it successfully, rather than pay it lip-service, requires an implicit belief in its underlying principles and assumptions although, as with all theories, it is possible to take and use the parts that you consider to be appropriate.

The humanistic theme continues in the next chapter, which sees its application to adult learning and looks in greater depth at some of its activities.

A SUMMARY OF **KEY POINTS**

> Humanism came about in the early 1960s as a response to the then dominant behaviourist and psycho-analytical perspectives, which discounted individual free will.

> Abraham Maslow and Carl Rogers were prominent figures in the humanist movement.

> Maslow's hierachy of needs stresses the intrinsic nature of motivation and the natural drive towards self-actualisation.

> Rogers believed that, given the right conditions, individuals are capable of controlling and directing their own lives rather than depending upon others.

> This is one of the principal beliefs that underpin a 'student-centred' approach to learning.

> The role of the teacher in this approach is that of facilitator and the relationship that is formed with learners is crucial in successfully fulfilling this role.

> Facilitation is concerned with process.

> John Heron's model of facilitation identifies six dimensions of process and suggests that facilitation styles fall into three possible modes: hierarchical, co-operative or autonomous.

> The style adopted by a facilitator is determined by the expertise and stage of development of the group.

> Summerhill School is an example of an educational institution which is committed to a humanistic approach and is organised and run according to humanistic principles.

> Assessment is about personal achievement and development and adopts an ipsative approach to referencing.

REFERENCES REFERENCES **REFERENCES** REFERENCES **REFERENCES** REFERENCES

Brandes, D and Ginnis, P (1986) *A guide to student-centred learning*. Oxford: Basil Blackwell.

Candy, PC (1987) Evolution, revolution or devolution: Increasing learner control in the instructional setting, in D Boud and V Griffin (eds) (1987) *Appreciating adults learning: From the learners' perspective*. London: Kogan Page.

Heron, J (1999) *The complete facilitators' handbook*. London: Kogan Page.

Hunter, D, Bailey, A and Taylor, B (1993) *The art of facilitation*. Auckland: Tandem Press.

Kirschenbaum, H and Landhenderson, V (1989) *The Carl Rogers reader*. New York: Houghton Mifflin.

Maslow, A (1954) *Motivation and personality*. New York: Harper.

Maslow, A (1968) *Towards a psychology of being* (2nd edn). New York: Van Nostrand-Reinhold.

Maslow, A (1971) *The farther reaches of human nature*. New York: Viking.

Neill, AS (1960) *Summerhill School: A radical approach to learning*. New York: St Martin's Griffin.

Rogers, C (1969) *Freedom to learn*. Columbus, Ohio: Charles E Merrill Publishing Company.

Rogers, C (1989) *On becoming a person*. Boston, New York: Houghton Mifflin.

Rogers, J (2007) *Adults learning* (5th edn). New York: McGraw-Hill.

7
Andragogy

Chapter overview and objectives

There is a view that the nature and characteristics of adult learners have particular implications for the learning process in which they engage. This chapter builds upon the previous chapter by exploring the concept of andragogy – a vision of adult learning based upon humanistic principles – and some of the practices it encourages.

When you have worked through this chapter you will be able to:

- identify Knowles' assumptions about the nature of adult learners which underpin the andragogical approach;
- describe the implications of these assumptions for practice;
- recognise the form and purpose of a learning contract and the characteristics it shares with an individual learning plan (ILP);
- describe the stages in successfully setting up and implementing a learning contract;
- acknowledge the significance of the process of negotiation within an andragogical approach to learning;
- identify different forms of negotiation and differentiate between what may and what may not be negotiable within a learning environment;
- describe Kolb's model of experiential learning;
- distinguish between different forms of experiential learning;
- manage experiential learning activities in a systematic fashion.

This chapter contributes to the following values and areas of professional knowledge as contained in the LLUK professional standards for teachers, tutors and trainers in the lifelong learning sector:

AS4, BS2, CS4, DS3

AK1.1, AK4.1, AK4.3, BK1.1, BK1.2, BK1.3, BK2.1, BK2.7, CK3.1

The andragogical approach to adult learning

Andragogy, a term which has been around since 1833 when it was first used by Alexander Kapp, a German schoolteacher, was popularised in the 1970s by Malcolm Knowles, who defines it as *the art and science of helping adults learn* (Knowles, 1990, p54). Knowles used the term to describe his own theory of adult learning which he based around *what we know from experience and research about the unique characteristics of adult learners*. His interest was first aroused when observing adults being taught in the same fashion as children, a practice he considered as wholly inappropriate. Such practice provided the focus of Knowles' early work in which he compared andragogy with pedagogy – the art and science of teaching children. This comparison later proved to be unhelpful and he subsequently withdrew from this position, citing andragogy as a potential general model of good practice.

Knowles considered adult learners to possess distinct characteristics. Reflect upon your own experiences of learning. Do you learn differently from the way you did when a child? Consider also the characteristics of your own learners. Do you consider them to be adults? If so, what are the characteristics they display? If not, what characteristics prevent them from coming into this category? See how your thoughts compare with those of Knowles outlined below.

In considering the nature of adult learners, Knowles initially identified four basic assumptions.

Self-concept

Self concept was described in Chapter 5 as *everyone has their own particular view of themselves and their situation*, so what is at issue here is how adult learners perceive themselves. Knowles considered different ways of defining 'adult' and dismissed biological (capable of reproduction), legal (voting rights) and social (perform adult roles) definitions in favour of a psychological perspective in which adulthood is defined as arriving at *a self-concept of being responsible for our own lives, of being self-directing* (1990, p57). Knowles considered that as a person matures, their self-concept moves from one of dependency towards that of a self-directed human being. Adults therefore need to be seen in this way and treated accordingly by others, resentment and resistance resulting if this is not the case. On returning to an educational environment, however, the conditioning of their school experience can cause them to revert to a dependent mode, a state which is at odds with their adult status. Knowles advocates the use of learning activities that help adult learners make this transition from dependency to self-directedness.

Experience

Age brings with it an accumulation of rich and varied experience which provides both a valuable resource for learning and a base upon which to relate new learning. Many of the activities used in adult education such as discussion, case studies and problem-solving activities tap into this pool of experience. Adults identify very strongly with their experiences; these form part of their identity and to acknowledge experience is to also acknowledge the person. To ignore experience, however, is equivalent to ignoring or rejecting the person. There is therefore a strong case for the use of experiential approaches to learning. Experience can also have a negative side to it as it can lead to habit and a closed mind.

Readiness to learn

Adults do not learn 'what they ought' but are ready to learn that which they see as necessary to maintain and enhance their lives. This is influenced by the developmental tasks performed as part of their social roles. Knowles cites the example of a girl who would not be ready to learn about infant nutrition or marital relationships while at school but would be very ready to learn about these things when she became engaged to be married.

Orientation to learning

Adults are life-centred in their orientation to learning. Accordingly, they do not learn 'subjects' but learn in order to complete tasks or solve problems. This learning demands an immediacy of results as tasks and problems need to be tackled now rather than on some distant future occasion. Postponed application is not an option.

These four original assumptions were first published in 1975 but a further two assumptions relating to motivation and the need to know were added in 1984 and 1989 respectively.

Motivation

While acknowledging that adults are responsive to some extrinsic motivators such as better jobs or higher salaries, Knowles maintained that as a person matures, the motivation to learn becomes internalised. Incentives such as increased job satisfaction, self-esteem and quality of life or just the need to keep growing and developing become more important in giving adults a reason to learn.

The need to know

Knowles was influenced by the work of Alan Tough, who regarded the majority of adult learning (80 per cent) as occurring through individual learning projects. Tough found that considerable energy was invested in weighing up the benefits of the proposed learning and the negative consequences of not engaging in it. Knowles surmised from this that adult learners need to be made aware of the need to know in order to commit fully to learning.

REFLECTIVE TASK

How do the above assumptions about the defining characteristics of adults compare with your own views? Do you think they apply to your learners or indeed to yourself, or are there some with which you disagree?

It is important to examine the assumptions we and others make as they form the basis for actions and behaviours. The above assumptions represent Knowles' views on the nature of adult learners and having identified these characteristics, his next step was to examine their implications for practice, devising what he called a *technology of teaching*. He arrived at a number of design elements associated with the learning process which he considered as taking account of the status of adult learners. These design elements emphasised the role of the teacher as facilitator and were reported under the following headings (Knowles, 1990, p119).

Climate

Knowles considers the effects of physical environment and organisational climate but his main concern is the human and interpersonal climate which, he maintains, needs to be in tune with the adult self-concept of self-direction. The key words here for Knowles are 'mutuality', 'respectful', 'collaborative' and 'informal'. Like Rogers, he regards the relationship between teacher and learner to be of great significance in influencing the learning process as a whole.

Planning

Planning is viewed as an exercise which is conducted jointly by learner and teacher. This is in keeping with the adult's perceived need for self-direction and ensures commitment to the planned learning. Knowles makes the point that the degree of commitment shown is proportional to the degree of input into the decision-making process. If planning is the exclusive preserve of the teacher and therefore regarded as being imposed, commitment is minimal. A mechanism for mutual planning therefore takes account of adult status and increases commitment to learning.

Diagnosis of needs

Sometimes, specific learning needs are uppermost in the mind of the learner and so are easily identifiable. This is not always the case, however, and occasionally some kind of structured activity is needed to help learners identify their own needs. Knowles considered that learning needs are most readily identified by using a model of the desired total outcome, expressed in terms of competencies, as a starting point. This model can be constructed by reference to three sources – the views of the learners themselves, the requirements of the organisation in which they work and the expectations that society might have of someone performing the particular role in question. Ideally the final model would be an amalgam of the views of all three sources, although Knowles recognised that tensions between these three perspectives may have to be resolved. By comparing the learner's present level of development or competence against this ideal model, learning needs can be identified. Knowles regards it as crucial to the process that it is the learner themselves who identifies this gap between where they are and where they need to be.

Formulation of objectives

Having identified needs, these should be expressed in a focused, structured manner and this can be achieved through the writing of objectives of some description. Knowles reviewed the different ways in which objectives might be written, citing the work of Mager, Taba, Houle and Tough, without arriving at a clear indication of which is most appropriate other than *perhaps these differences in viewpoint on objectives are partly reconcilable by assigning the more terminal-behaviour-oriented procedures to training and the more inquiry-process-oriented procedures to education* (1990, p132). What is plain, however, is that regardless of the style of objective employed, they should be devised as far as possible by learners themselves and be seen as relevant to the previously identified learning needs.

Design and activities

In an andragogical model the design of a learning programme is based not around content but around learning needs identified by learners and expressed in objective form. The main design task is to choose and sequence an appropriate set of activities to address these. The chosen activities would normally be experiential in nature. Knowles acknowledges that the underpinning philosophy of self-direction in his approach places a large degree of responsibility for learning on the learner. This may invoke a degree of culture-shock in instances where previous experience may have conditioned learners into teacher dependency. He suggests the use of preparatory activities to address this.

Evaluation

Knowles considers the main function of evaluation not to be that of examining the quality of the provision, but rather a process of re-examining and reformulating learning needs. As he explains:

If every learning experience is to lead to further learning, as continuing education implies, then every evaluation process should include some provisions for helping the learner re-examine their models of desired competencies and reassess the discrepancies between the model and their newly developed levels of competencies.

(Knowles, 1990, p138)

In order to be considered true adult education, all of the above should be approached as joint enterprises between teacher and learner. Knowles cites activities such as planning, negotiation, needs diagnosis and re-diagnosis as 'mutual' pursuits.

REFLECTIVE TASK

The above spell out a role of the teacher which is very different from the more traditional teacher-led approach with which you may be familiar. Do you think this role could be adopted either wholly or in part within your present working environment? Where would any constraints arise?

Contract learning

Knowles recognised the need for a structure of some kind to convert his design elements from statements of intent into actual practice. He suggests that all of the above components can be subsumed into a single process known as a learning contract; the drawing up of an agreement between the learner and facilitator specifying the learning which is to take place and how it will be accomplished and measured.

Although originally introduced specifically into the arena of adult learning by Knowles, learning contracts are now becoming much more widespread in both use and popularity. They can be incorporated into almost any learning programme in any curriculum area and are being used more extensively in all sectors of education as, if properly implemented, they are regarded as having a number of potential advantages over other learning strategies.

Learning contracts are seen as motivational, bringing relevance to the learning process by matching the learning to be undertaken to previously identified learning needs. Motivation is further enhanced by learner participation in devising the contract, although care must be taken at this stage to ensure clarity in both thought and the recording of the contract, as ambiguity or vagueness can lead to frustration at a later date. The use of learning contracts helps develop the skills of independent learning, particularly those relating to time management, planning and decision-making.

Because of this increase in popularity over a number of different learning contexts, a variety of different approaches to the use of learning contracts have emerged. According to Boak (1998, p5), however:

All learning contracts, however loosely the term is applied, share certain characteristics: a degree of choice for the learner, a learning plan and (usually) an agreement between the learner and someone who will help them – a tutor, trainer, coach or mentor.

An example of a format is shown on the next page.

Learning Contract

Course: ....

Name ....

1. What are you going to learn
   (State learning objectives using SMART terminology)

2. How will you achieve this?
   (List the strategies you will employ)

3. What will you need?
   (Identify any resources you think you will need)

4. How will you know that you have been successful in your learning?
   (Describe how you will evidence that learning has taken place)

5. By what date will you have completed this contract?
   (Identify a realistic target date for completion)

Signed .... (Learner)   Date: ....

Signed .... (Tutor)   Date: ....

In many respects, a learning contract bears comparison with an individual learning plan (ILP). The Quality Improvement Agency (QIA), now part of the Learning and Skills Improvement Service (LSIS), suggests that ILPs *form a 'route map' of how a learner will get from their starting point on a learning journey to the desired end point*. The Learning and Skills Council (LSC) requires an ILP to be completed for each learner enrolled on a course that they fund. A typical ILP format is shown below and the similarities between this and a learning contract can be seen.

Individual Learning Plan				
Objective (expressed in 'SMART' terms)	What needs to be done to achieve this objective	Evidence of achievement	By when	Review date

Name: ....

Signed ....   Date: ....

Tutor signature ....   Date: ....

Although the formats above may be considered self-explanatory to a certain extent, the success of a learning contract or an ILP is not guaranteed merely by completing the document. It is the process behind and beyond this that determines whether or not the learning contract or ILP will achieve its purpose.

The steps outlined below refer to the setting up and completing of a learning contract but could equally well be applied to an ILP.

1. Preparation of learners

A learning contract is learner-centred in nature and so it is expected that it is the learner rather than the teacher will make the bigger contribution to setting up the contract in the first place and who will bear the ultimate responsibility for doing the work required to ensure successful completion. This is no small undertaking and so, other than practical matters such as organising a suitable time and environment in which to meet, and preparing a suitable contract format, the teacher's initial contribution lies in preparing the learner for the task in hand. Learners are being asked to make a considerable investment in terms of time and effort and so need to be confident that results will justify this investment.

Boak (1998, p43) suggests that learners need to be 'primed' before entering into a learning contract to ensure an effective outcome. Priming consists of:

- explaining the purpose of a learning contract and the form it takes;
- establishing relevance and building confidence in using the approach and its ability to reach a useful and practical outcome;
- clarifying exactly what the learner is expected to do.

This is particularly important when learners are unfamiliar with the notion of a learning contract. Talking through instances of successful applications of learning contracts and having relatively straightforward examples of completed contracts to hand may prove useful at this stage.

2. Agreement on the content of the learning contract

Having put learners into a receptive frame of mind and made sure they understand exactly what is required of them, the next stage is to agree the content of the contract. As the whole process is based around fulfilling individual needs, the first stage is to clarify exactly what these are and to express them in a clear and unambiguous manner as previously described. Subsequent decisions should flow naturally from this stage and so it is worth spending some time in getting it right. As well as establishing the desired outcomes it is important to establish criteria by which a judgment can be made as to whether or not these have been successfully achieved. The exact nature and level of formality of these criteria will depend upon the purpose of the contract; is it concerned with personal development or is it being used in part fulfilment of the requirements of a qualification? The latter will require a more substantial and concrete evidence base than the former.

The goal of this stage of the process is to arrive at a learning contract which is not only relevant and useful but is also realistic and achievable within whatever constraints that might exist. Thus, although the greater the learner input, the greater the commitment to the success of the contract, a successful outcome may require a number of teacher interventions that guide learners towards the making of appropriate and practical decisions. Arriving at a completed contract is achieved through a process of facilitation and negotiation. The level of intervention will differ from learner to learner depending upon their confidence, level of independence and familiarity with this type of approach. Reference back to Heron's model of facilitation in Chapter 6 may help here as it is crucial that the balance between teacher and learner input is maintained in such a manner that the learner is left with a feeling that it is 'their' learning contract.

3. Monitoring progress and providing support

Support can take a number of forms such as providing a sounding board for ideas, guidance on sources of information, reassurance on progress to date or the maintenance of motivation levels. It can be provided from a distance by telephone or email contact but an agreed time and place to meet for actual face-to-face contact is the approach that most learners generally welcome. Sometimes, particularly in the early stages, this can take place as a group meeting with other learners who are also engaged in contract learning, when the main area of discussion may well revolve around the process. The feelings of mutual support and camaraderie that can be generated by such meetings can have a very positive effect on motivation and morale. Generally, however, as work on the contract progresses, a more individual approach will be favoured as content becomes more of a focus. At the conclusion of a meeting an agreed target or action plan should be negotiated in preparation for the next meeting.

4. Evaluation of results

Formative mutual evaluation will be a natural ongoing process throughout the life of the contract. It will contribute to the learning process as a whole and also to the shape of the final outcome. Summative evaluation is also required, however. If the learning contract is to be used to count towards a qualification, it needs to be checked against the requirements of the qualification even though it may be a complete piece of work in its own right. A slightly different approach can be adopted if the learning contract serves a personal development function, but here also there are questions to be answered. Has the contract reached completion? Has it served its purpose? What has been learned both from the outcome and process of the contract? Where does it lead to next?

Negotiation/planning

On the assumption that adult learners are to some extent self-determining and therefore willing to take on increasing responsibility for their own learning, much of the planning in an andragogical approach is based around the facilitation of individual needs and this has been the focus of this chapter so far. In most institutions, however, the main form of contact between teachers and learners takes place in a group setting. Nonetheless, this does not preclude an andragogical approach as the principles explored so far can also be applied to a group setting. It is possible for instance, to set up group learning contracts and it is certainly possible to engage in negotiation, a key skill in an andragogical approach, at group level as well as on an individual basis.

Negotiation is far from being a new concept within fields such as management and industrial relationships and within such contexts can be defined as:

A process through which parties move from their initially divergent positions to a point where agreement may be reached.

(Steele and Beasor, 1999, p3)

When taking an educational perspective, however, negotiation is more a reflection of *the rights of the subjects to have a say in planning curricula* (Kelly, 1987, p61). This is a concept which is not limited to adult education, however, as can be seen from the following quote taken from a textbook on teaching in the middle years.

Research suggests that students' learning is more effective and rewarding if they have a 'voice' in and ownership of aspects of the curriculum and the teaching/ learning process.

(Bahr and Pendergast, 2005, p164)

REFLECTIVE TASK

Before reading any further, consider the groups you teach. Do you think some form of negotiation would prove beneficial to their learning? If so, how would you carry this out? If not, what do you see as the main disadvantages or barriers?

The process of negotiation finds support from both the humanist perspective in general and from the andragogical perspective in particular (Hillier, 2005, p94). In citing arguments in favour of such an approach Neary, (2002, p113) suggests that:

• adult learners are the best people to decide their own educational needs;
• adult learners can bring considerable experience of their own to the educational situation;
• it can motivate learners;
• learners should have the freedom not to be told what they should study.

Invariably, particularly in light of Neary's last point, thoughts initially turn to course content as an area for negotiation. After all, if content is negotiated it must be pertinent and relevant to the group of learners and should address their needs in a fairly direct manner. This is an appealing scenario but the negotiation of course content is not quite so straightforward. There are two main stumbling blocks.

• Groups rarely have sufficient knowledge and experience of the content related to the subject to be able to make informed choices. Many learners feel this is a case of putting the cart before the horse as they cannot say what they need to know because the subject is new to them, so they do not yet know what it is that they do not know.
• Choices may well be constrained or even nonexistent due to the inflexibility of the syllabus to be followed and perhaps it is the case that rather than negotiate content, *there is an external body of knowledge and skills to which learners should be introduced* (Neary, 2002, p113).

In reality, content is probably the most difficult area to negotiate. As negotiation normally occurs at or near the beginning of a course, learners are potentially confronted with two areas – course content and the process of negotiation – which may cause them problems. Much easier to negotiate would be the ground rules which the group will work to and this could serve as a gentler introduction to this way of working. This is a well accepted manner of arriving at ground rules, to which groups are generally more committed having devised them themselves. Even simpler and more straightforward as a negotiation 'starter' is the timing of breaks. Content is only one aspect of a course that can be negotiated and as Boud et al. (1985, p159) suggest, negotiation should include *both the 'what' and 'how' of the curriculum.*

If content is regarded as the 'what', the 'how' of negotiation might include:

- priority, order and structure of content;
- types of methods and activities to be used;
- balance of teacher-led and learner-led activity;
- approaches to assessment;
- evaluation procedures;
- attendance requirements;
- aspects of the physical environment such as room layout;
- start, finish and break times.

The list can be fairly endless but is it possible or even desirable to negotiate everything? In terms of what can and cannot be negotiated, a continuum of negotiation would have 'blank-sheet' negotiation at one end where anything and everything is party to negotiation, and prescription at the other where negotiation is negligible. In between these two extremes lie the possibilities of a more structured approach or perhaps a menu of choices, as shown below.

Negotiation continuum

A structured approach involves the setting down of parameters or limits within which the negotiation is to be conducted; and a menu approach, normally used with groups who require some guidance, offers a number of choices from a given list.

Wherever the real-life negotiation process fits along this continuum, in order to be successful it must state its position with respect to exactly what is negotiable and what is a given. As Boomer et al. (1992, p288) suggest, *hard headed judgements are made about what can and cannot be done.* The determining factors on where the parameters of the negotiation will be set include:

- flexibility of programme and syllabus;
- culture of the organisation;
- attitudes of the teacher;
- knowledge, experience and cohesion of the group.

The last of these points also has a bearing on how the negotiation might be carried out and the teacher will need to make a judgment on the readiness of the group to engage meaningfully in the activity of negotiation.

It may be that the maturity of the group dictates a gradual approach. Simple things may be negotiated initially as a matter of course without ever making direct reference to or formalising the process. As familiarity and confidence increase, the scope and level of negotiation can also increase until learners are sufficiently comfortable with the process for a more formal statement of intent to be made and negotiation to be carried out in a more transparent manner. Daines, Daines and Graham (2006, p46) suggest that an approach to be used with less confident groups could include an initial mix of consultation, where *the tutor checks things out with the group but retains the option of whether or not to modify his/ her initial proposal*, on the more difficult issues such as content, and negotiation on the simpler, more practical aspects of the course.

If, with a well-formed, more experienced and knowledgeable group, the decision is to take a more apparent and formal approach, the first stage in the process is to come to an agreement with the group concerning the reasons for and the value of the proposed negotiation as well as the specific procedures to be followed. The second stage is, as described above, to make explicit what can be negotiated and what is set in stone and therefore not negotiable. Once the scene is set in this way, the negotiation itself can take place.

REFLECTIVE TASK

Some form of negotiation is possible with all groups and can have an effect even if conducted in a very limited fashion. Consider the groups that you teach and pick out two – the one with whom negotiation is most possible and the group with whom negotiation is least possible. For each, identify what can be negotiated and think about how best to organise this in each case.

Experiential learning

Knowles suggests that the methods best employed with adults fall under the general heading of experiential learning as adults prefer a problem-centred approach to learning and generally learn best when what is to be learned is presented within a context of real life.

Defining experiential learning is not as straightforward as it might at first seem. There is, for instance, considerable academic debate over the difference between learning from experience and experiential learning. Weil and McGill (1989, p3) classify experiential learning in terms of four villages of practice, each relating to different meaning, aims and sets of values. For the purposes of this chapter, however, experiential learning will be considered as:

> *the sense-making process of active engagement between the inner world of the person and the outer world of the environment.*
>
> (Beard and Wilson, 2006, p2)

This definition is in keeping with Kolb's model of experiential learning encountered in the Introduction to this book. As with any cycle, it can be entered at any point but generally it is considered that the first stage is to engage in some form of concrete experience (the outer world of the environment) which is then processed (the sense-making process) by the individual (engagement between the inner world of the person) in order to arrive at some form of learning which will inform future practice.

Experience falls into two main categories. The first of these concerns 'real-life'. Learning is initiated by partaking in or fully immersing oneself in a real-life experience in the here-and-now, allowing learning through the senses to take place. This is the type of experience advocated by Kolb. Jarvis (1995) terms this a 'primary experience' and suggests that *secondary experiences such as those which have occurred in the past but can be relived in the mind – 'there and then' rather than 'here and now' – can also form the basis of experiential learning.*

There is, however, a limit to what can be experienced at first hand and the second category consists of 'manufactured' experiences which simulate or take the place of real-life experiences. Kolb (1984, p9) suggests that activities such as internships, field placements, work/study assignments, structured exercises, role plays and gaming simulations fall into this category.

Dennison and Kirk (1990) devised the 'do, review, learn, apply' model shown below.

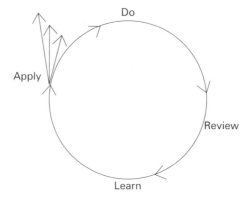

(Dennison and Kirk, 1990)

The different arrows arising from the 'Apply' stage reflect the variety of different situations in which skills and knowledge can be applied as well as the possibility of linking one learning cycle to the next. Although the stages are similar to Kolb's model, the Dennison and Kirk model limits the experience to the manufactured type already identified, describing it as *some shared experience for all students organised by a tutor* (1990, p18). They suggest that while the first two stages can be influenced or even controlled by the teacher, the two subsequent stages are internal to the learner and therefore beyond influence or control.

Borton (1970, p89) provides an even simpler model based around three simple questions:

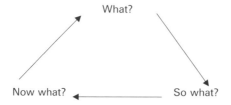

The common feature in all of these models is that they include some form of experience and a series of steps through which the experience is processed in some way in order to extract learning from it.

Review your own teaching and identify any activities that you currently use that you would consider to be 'experiential' in nature. How do these activities fit with the models described above? What are their common features that make them 'experiential'?

Kolb's model of experiential learning has been the subject of considerable criticism. Critical comment mainly concerns the related learning style inventory produced by Kolb, but the experiential cycle itself attracts criticism for its sequential approach as *in reality, these things may be happening all at once* (Jeffs and Smith, 2005, p65) and its individual approach, which leads to a narrow viewpoint as it precludes other factors that influence learning.

The model itself, however, can still provide a guide to practice. Tennant (1988, p105) argues that:

> *These objections do not preclude the possibility of using the experiential learning model to inform adult education practice. As a rule of thumb the model provides an excellent framework for planning teaching and learning activities.*

Gibbs (1988, p23), for instance, describes a series of practical methods for the implementation of the experiential learning cycle under the headings:

- planning for experience;
- increasing awareness of experience;
- reviewing and reflecting upon experience;
- providing substitute experiences.

Knowles et al. (1998, p147) used Kolb's model to try to classify the different forms of experiential exercise, matching each against the stages of Kolb's cycle. An extended version of his work is given below.

Kolb's stage	Strategy
Concrete experience	Simulation, case study, field trip, real experience, demonstration, examples, games, trigger films
Reflective observation	Discussion, small groups, buzz groups, designated observers, logs, journals, brainstorming, questions
Abstract conceptualisation	Sharing content, analogies, introduction of theories, model building
Active experimentation	Laboratory experiences, on-the-job experience, internships, practice sessions, projects, homework, simulations

Kolb's cycle can also be used to adopt a systematic approach to managing experiential activities, as described below.

Managing experiential learning activities

Assuming a starting point of concrete experience within Kolb's cycle, the first stage in managing an experiential approach is to establish an experience appropriate to the envisaged learning. This is the 'doing' part of the cycle. If real-life experience can be drawn upon, this is probably the best option, but failing that a number of activities can be considered. If the proposed learning is knowledge-related, case studies, problem-solving exercises or some form of game may be the preferred alternative. Skills-based learning is better suited to activities such as demonstration, practical exercise or simulation whereas if attitude change is the desired result, discussion, debate or role play will prove more effective. Whichever activity is chosen, it should be managed in a manner that focuses on the main learning points to be explored. It may be necessary to allocate roles and for some to act as observers, in which case specific 'watch-points' should be established. It is important that everyone should have some kind of active part to play as it is the experience itself which is important at this stage. Wholehearted participation and immersion in the experience by all is the goal at this point.

Upon completion of the activity, participants are asked to look back upon and review what has taken place, identifying significant 'happenings' within the activity as a whole. The aim is to establish a clear picture of 'what' has occurred prior to engaging in analysis. This can be achieved by:

- asking for thoughts and contributions, limiting these to what happened;
- observers giving feedback to others on what they saw;
- everyone writing a short, factual report and then comparing findings.

It can also be achieved by any activity which involves a replaying of the experience in the mind to establish the answers to questions such as: What were the significant facts/features? What particularly stood out?

The time has now come for some analysis or 'abstract conceptualisation', as Kolb prefers to call it. This stage answers the questions concerning 'why' – why did it happen this way? What are the reasons for . . .? It is a process of trying to make some sense of what happened and involves the interpretation of events and uncovering and understanding the relationships between them. It is only after this that strategies for future use can be devised. This sense-making process may involve learners in:

- breaking the experience down into its constituent parts;
- sharing thoughts and ideas;
- drawing on previous experience in order to make comparisons;
- looking to appropriate models and theory to provide a framework for analysis.

The teacher's task at this point is to prevent discussions heading down blind alleys and to suggest, explain and clarify thinking on appropriate theories or models which may prove useful in arriving at an understanding.

If the three previous stages have been successfully completed, learners will now have acquired sufficient knowledge and understanding to be able to formulate ways in which they can take what they have learned from this experience and put it into practice. 'Active experimentation' involves exactly what it says. Arriving at a plan of action, informed by reflection and analysis, and testing it out in a relevant context. This is the 'doing' stage. Teachers can help learners at this stage to think through and mentally evaluate the decisions they have arrived at, perhaps suggesting situations and scenarios for this purpose. Finally an action plan should be devised specifying a specific situation and time for putting the action into practice 'for real'.

Finally

Andragogy can be considered as a particular application of a student-centred approach. Certainly it shares many of the ideas proposed by Rogers, particularly those of the learner taking control of their own learning and the role of facilitator adopted by the teacher.

The concept of andragogy is not without its critics although none appears to have offered a practical alternative. A summary of their views is given by Merriam, Caffarella and Baumgartner (2007, pp85–90).

- It is unclear as to whether andragogy constitutes a theory of teaching, a theory of learning or a series of principles of good practice.
- Several of its assumptions are problematical.
- It ignores the social context within which learning takes place.
- It is culturally and politically specific.

Andragogy has nonetheless had a big impact on adult education and *practitioners who work with adult learners continue to find Knowles's Andragogy, with its characteristics of adult learners, to be a helpful rubric for better understanding adults as learners* (Merriam, et al., 2007, p92).

A SUMMARY OF **KEY POINTS**

> The term 'andragogy' was popularised by Malcolm Knowles in the 1970s and means 'the art and science of helping adults to learn'.

> Andragogical theory is based upon a number of assumptions that Knowles made concerning the nature of adult learners. These assumptions relate to the adult's need to know, self-concept, store of experience, readiness and orientation to learning.

> Knowles derived a technology of teaching containing a number of design elements from his assumptions.

> The design elements of Knowles' approach can be encapsulated in a single approach based on the use of a learning contract.

> The current practice of using individual learning plans (ILPs) shares a number of features with the use of learning contracts.

> The process of setting up and implementing a learning contract includes the four stages of preparation of learners, agreement on the content of the learning contract, monitoring progress and providing support and evaluation of results.

> Negotiation is a fundamental activity in an andragogical approach to learning and has the effect of increasing learner commitment. It can take a number of different forms which reflect the degree of decision-making which is open to learners.

> Negotiation can cover a range of areas relating to the 'what' and the 'how' of the curriculum.

> Andragogy suggests that the learning activities from which adult learners derive the most benefit are experiential in nature.

> Experiences must be processed in order for learning to occur and Kolb's model of experiential learning identifies the stages involved in this process and the sequence in which they occur.

> Experience can be real or simulated and Kolb's model provides a systematic approach to managing activities involving either type of experience.

REFERENCES REFERENCES **REFERENCES** REFERENCES REFERENCES REFERENCES

Bahr, N and Pendergast, D (2005) *Teaching middle years: Rethinking curriculum pedagogy and assessment*. Hove, Sussex: Allen and Unwin.

Beard, C and Wilson, JP (2006) *Experiential learning: A best practice handbook for educators and trainers* (2nd edn). London: Kogan Page.

Boak, G (1998) *A complete guide to learning contracts.* Aldershot: Gower.

Boomer, G, Lester, N, Onore, C and Cook, J (eds) (1992) *Negotiating the curriculum.* London: Routledge Falmer.

Borton, T (1970) *Reach, touch and teach: Student concerns and process education*. New York: McGraw-Hill.

Boud, D, Keogh, R and Walker, D (1985) *Reflection: Turning experience into learning*. London: Routledge.

Daines, J, Daines, C and Graham, B (2006) *Adult learning, adult teaching* (4th edn). Cardiff: Welsh Academic Press.

Dennison, B and Kirk, R (1990) *Do, review, learn, apply: A simple guide to experiential learning.* Oxford: Blackwell Education.

Gibbs, G (1988) *Learning by doing; A guide to teaching and learning methods*. London: Further Education Unit.

Hillier, Y (2005) *Reflective teaching in further and adult education* (2nd edn). London, New York: Continuum.

Jarvis, P (1995) *Adult and continuing education: Theory and practice.* London: Routledge.

Jeffs, T and Smith, M (2005) *Informal education* (3rd edn). Nottingham: Educational Heretics Press.

Kelly, AV (1987) *Education.* London: Heinneman.

Knowles, M (1990) *The adult learner: A neglected species* (4th edn). Houston: Gulf Publishing Company.

Knowles M, Holton, E and Swanson, R (1998) *The adult learner* (5th edn). Woburn MA: Butterworth-Heinemann.

Kolb, D (1984) *Experiential learning: Experience as the source of learning and development.* New Jersey: Prentice-Hall.

Merriam, S, Caffarella, R and Baumgartner, L (2007) *Learning in adulthood: A comprehensive guide* (3rd edn). San Francisco: Jossey Bass.

Neary, M (2002) *Curriculum studies in post-compulsory and adult education*. Cheltenham: Nelson Thornes.

Steele, P and Beasor, T (1999) *Business negotiation: A practical workbook*. Farnham: Gower Publishing.

Tennant, M (1988) *Psychology and adult learning*. London and New York: Routledge.

Weil, S and McGill, I (eds) (1989) *Making sense of experiential learning*. Milton Keynes: Open University Press.

8
Attention, perception and learning

Information processing theory, which compares the working of the mind with that of a computer, is one area of research within the field of cognitive psychology. It attempts to account for the ways in which people receive, store, integrate, retrieve and use information through the processes of attention, perception and memory. This chapter examines the first two of these processes and looks at ways in which they can be promoted during teaching.

When you have worked through this chapter you will be able to:

- describe what is meant by information processing theory;
- recognise the selective nature of the process of attention;
- identify the reasons as to why some stimuli are selected rather than others;
- recognise the importance of attention within the learning process;
- describe the factors influencing the relative ease or difficulty of dividing attention between two or more tasks;
- identify strategies which can be used to attract and maintain learner attention;
- describe the individual nature of perception;
- describe the role played by previous experience in the process of perception;
- recognise strategies that can be used to shape and assist learners' perceptions;
- identify the role of language in perception.

This chapter contributes to the following values and areas of professional knowledge as contained in the LLUK professional standards for teachers, tutors and trainers in the lifelong learning sector:

AS4, BS2, CS4, DS3

AK1.1, AK4.1, AK4.3, BK1.1, BK1.2, BK1.3, BK2.1, BK2.7, CK3.1

Information processing theory

Due to its abstract nature, cognitive psychology makes frequent use of metaphors and analogies in order to make its various concepts, principles and theories more understandable and accessible. Information processing theory, one branch of cognitive psychology, makes use of an analogy which compares the brain with a computer in the way in which it processes information. According to this approach, information from the environment is acted upon by a series of processing systems, each of which transforms or changes the information in some way, resulting in an appropriate response.

REFLECTIVE TASK

Analogies make a comparison between two different objects or processes in order to explain a difficult or abstract idea by showing how it is similar in some way to something with which we are familiar.

Although useful, analogies have their limitations and are sometimes thought to be over-simplistic. How effective do you think this analogy of the computer and the brain is? In what ways do you think it is useful? What do you consider its major limitations to be?

Some of the terms used in information processing theory are explained below and may help you in clarifying your response to the above task.

- Serial processing – one process has to be completed before the next starts.
- Parallel processing – some or even all processes occur at the same time.
- Bottom-up processing – the initial stimulus initiates and drives the process.
- Top-down processing – previous knowledge or information which influences interpretation of the initial stimulus is the biggest influence on the process.

One obvious difference between the computer and the brain lies in the type of processing of which each is capable. Computers are serial processors, completing one process before commencing the next. Humans, on the other hand, often engage in more than one task simultaneously. We can walk and talk at the same time for instance, so the brain, although sometimes acting as a serial processor, is also capable of parallel processing.

The computer always reacts to the same input in exactly the same manner. Life would be rather confusing for computer users if this was not the case. This means that the computer is a bottom-up processor. It is the input or initial stimulus that determines the direction that subsequent processing will take. This can also be true for humans. A red traffic light would hopefully trigger the same response in everyone who saw it. If, however, the stimulus object was a dog, different people may well react in a different manner depending upon their previous experience of dogs. Thus on some occasions, we may well react differently to a given stimulus and at an individual level we might even react differently to the same stimulus on different occasions. In such instances, it is our interpretation of the stimulus rather than its specific characteristics that determines how it is processed. The brain therefore can act either as a bottom-up or a top-down processor.

The computer analogy thus presents a rather simpler view of the human brain than is actually the case. The most recent approach to studying the processes taking place in the brain, known as cognitive neuroscience, involves an examination of the biological and neurological aspects of the brain in order to better understand how it functions. It attempts to identify the biological underpinning of the various mental processes, achieving this by scanning the brain in a variety of different ways to locate the specific regions of the brain which are involved in each. Whichever approach is favoured, however, the processes under study remain the same and it is three of these – attention, perception and memory – along with their implications for teaching and learning, which form the focus of the next two chapters.

Attention

Like the computer, the mind has a limited capacity for the amount and nature of the information it can process. In the same way that a computer will crash if asked to perform too many tasks simultaneously, the brain suffers from overload if asked to process too many stimuli at the same time. The purpose of the attention phase of information processing is to prevent such overload by filtering out the majority of presented stimuli, allowing only those which are selected to proceed to the next phase of the process. The most definitive and most often-quoted statement concerning attention is that of William James (1890, pp403–4), who wrote that:

> *It is the taking of possession by the mind, in clear and vivid form, of one out of what seem several simultaneously possible objects or trains of thought. Focalisation, concentration of consciousness are of its essence. It implies withdrawal of some things in order to deal effectively with others.*

Attention then refers to the way in which information is processed in a selective manner. One question raised by this viewpoint relates to what it is that determines which stimuli are selected and which are not. The study of this aspect of attention is known as focused attention or bottleneck theory and different theorists within this field supply different answers to the above question.

REFLECTIVE TASK

Before you read any further, reflect back on your day so far. What has particularly caught your attention up to now? Make a list of these 'attention grabbers' and next to each write down why it was successful in gaining your attention.

Focused attention

One view of focused attention is presented by Broadbent's filter theory. As its name suggests, Broadbent's theory proposes that when a number of stimuli are presented simultaneously, because of the limited capacity of the brain to cope with all of these, most are filtered out and only the remaining selected stimulus proceeds to the next stage of processing. The mechanism by which Broadbent suggested this filtering process takes place is illustrated below.

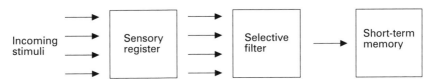

Two or more stimuli presented at the same time (parallel processing) gain simultaneous access to the sensory register. This is a kind of sensory memory which retains an impression of the stimulus long enough to enable a decision to be made regarding further processing. This particular phenomenon is demonstrated when you write your name against the sky with a sparkler on bonfire night. You will see an image of your name rather than a series of points of light. This suggests that that the different images formed by the different positions of the sparkler persist for a short while, hence you fleetingly see your name. Similarly, watching television would be far less satisfying without sensory memory as you would see a series of still pictures instead of a continuously moving image, as the persistence of the still images allows them to overlap, forming the illusion of a single, constantly changing image. Sensory stimuli then, are held for a short period of time in the sensory register before being processed. Any stimuli that are not selected for further processing in this time period will disappear. As Broadbent (quoted in Naatanen, 1992, p30) states:

> *part of the information from this buffer store [sensory register] will fail to pass this stage of serial processing before the time limit on the buffer store expires and those items that are lost in this way will have no further effect on behaviour.*

As only sensory memories are captured, the filter selects one of these inputs on the basis of its physical characteristics, passing it on (serial processing) to the short-term memory for further processing.

Attention is an important part of the learning process, so much so that:

> *they [teachers] have to use cueing signals to direct attention, develop learning materials and tasks that are stimulating and interesting, use strong colours and sounds, and maintain variety of task and approach.*
>
> (Bartlett and Burton, 2007, p120)

So what does Broadbent's theory tell us about attention in the learning environment? It suggests that it is the physical characteristics of the actual stimulus that are responsible for attracting attention. An example of this would be Bartlett and Burton's 'strong colours and sounds'. The intensity and nature of a stimulus have a strong bearing on whether or not it will be selectively attended to. Examples of this are as follows.

- Some colours are more likely to attract attention than others. Generally red is a good attracter of attention, which is why we use it to denote danger. The greater the intensity of the stimulus – the brighter the colour, the louder the sound, the stronger the smell or taste, the greater the pressure of touch – the more likely it is to attract attention.
- When a cat stalks a bird, it is as still as possible. It knows that sudden or prolonged movement will catch the attention of the bird and it will fly away. Variety in stimulus attracts attention. A police siren, as well as being high pitched and loud (intensity), is also irregular. Variety in learning activity, switching the focus from teacher to learner and use of resource switching from written to graphical, will help in maintaining attention throughout a session of learning. The reverse is also true. Monotony will not capture attention. Reliance on one particular activity, for instance, particularly if passive in nature, and a voice that does not vary in pitch or intonation gives ample evidence of this.
- Anything which is different and so stands out from its surroundings will attract attention. Underlining, colour and different styles of print such as capital letters, bold or italic type are often used to achieve this effect.
- It is useful to highlight and focus learner attention on items which are particularly important or less obvious using verbal cues or attention pointers. If using explanation, cues such as *you should note that...*, *importantly*, *crucially* can be used. With a more visual approach such as demonstration, cues such as *watch how I...*, *see how the...* or *note the point at which...* can be used to direct attention in the required direction.
- Under normal circumstances, we take in most sensory information from our environment through our eyes. The task in which we are engaged will have an obvious influence on the degree of use of each of the individual senses (e.g. potters rely more than most on touch, cooks on taste and smell, musicians on hearing), but generally the majority of our contact with the external environment is through sight. Petty (1998, p315) suggests that sight is responsible for 87 per cent of the information that enters the brain, hearing for 9 per cent and only 4 per cent for the remaining senses. We have, therefore, a great appetite for visual stimulation. Consequently, visual aids are an invaluable tool in attracting and maintaining attention and if some of the characteristics above are taken into account in their design, their effectiveness can be even further enhanced. Some of the more useful visual design techniques (Francis and Gould, 2009, p127) are illustrated below.

Visual Techniques

1. **Use**
2. **numbers**
3. **to**
4. **give**
5. **structure**

BIG / small

↑

Visual 'puns'

SUB – HEADINGS
to create order

Different letter size for

Headings

Use the

DAILY NEWS

technique

Bullets can be used for lists
- Item 1
- Item 2

Emphasise through
Bold
Italic
Underline
CAPITALS

Striking layout

Frame ideas

REFLECTIVE TASK

Look back to the list you made in the last reflective task of things that attracted your attention. How many of them provide examples of Broadbent's theory because their attraction was related to their physical characteristics? Do you have other items on your list that do not fall into this category? If so, why do you think they particularly attracted your attention?

In 1953, Cherry described what he called the 'cocktail effect'. This is the situation that occurs when, in a crowded room, an individual can focus on one conversation among the many that are taking place. This phenomenon could be said to support Broadbent's theory on the grounds that the voice that a person is attending to has different physical characteristics from those of other people in the room. However, if, whilst involved in and focusing attention on this one conversation, your name is mentioned in a different conversation on the other side of the room, your attention will invariably switch to the other conversation. This last instance does not fit with Broadbent's theory, which has also been found wanting in a number of other ways. This prompted Treisman to propose a modified form of Broadbent's theory which suggested that selection was influenced by factors other than solely the physical characteristics of the stimulus. Treisman's model is illustrated below.

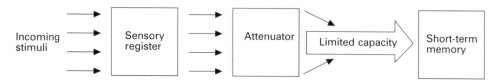

Broadbent's is an all-or-nothing type of model in that stimuli which are not selected are lost. Treisman suggested that although physical characteristics lead to initial selection, rather than being lost, the non-selected stimuli are attenuated; they are adjusted or 'turned down' rather like turning down the volume control on a radio. All stimuli pass on to the next stage but in their new attenuated state. The stimuli next pass on to a limited-capacity channel within which different threshold or acceptance levels exist for these attenuated stimuli. Those which have a personal relevance (such as your name) have a high likelihood of being attended to and various other contextual characteristics also increase the likelihood of attention. Whereas Broadbent suggests a bottom-up approach to selection of stimuli for attention, Treisman's attenuation theory includes elements of top-down processing as well, giving rise to a more individual approach to attention. The Bartlett and Burton quote on strategies used by teachers to attract and maintain attention, talks of *tasks that are stimulating and interesting*. What constitutes 'stimulating and interesting' will differ from person to person and Treisman gives us some insight into this. Attenuation Theory suggests attention is attracted and maintained through a number of elements.

- Personal significance – this encompasses anything that relates directly to us or our current areas of interest. Someone with an interest in birds will hear the first cuckoo call of spring, whereas for others this will just be part of the background noise that remains unattended to. Attitudes and prejudices will also come into play here; some things will be dismissed out of hand while others will merit further attention.
- Expectations – attention is naturally drawn to anything that lies outside of our expectations. The unusual, the novel or anything that seems out of place to us is always worthy of closer attention.
- Curiosity – a form of intrinsic motivation which, if aroused, will attract attention to those stimuli which contribute to its satisfaction. One way of arousing curiosity is by posing questions at the beginning of a teaching session or presenting information which would appear to contradict what is already known.

REFLECTIVE TASK

Does Treisman's attenuation theory account for the unexplained 'attention grabbers' from your previous list? Can you relate these in some way to yourself or your individual perceptions?

A third approach to attention has been suggested by Deutsch and Deutsch. They were of the opinion that filtering or selection took place only after all stimuli were fully analysed for meaning. Stimuli were then chosen on the basis of relevance or pertinence to the task in hand.

All three of these theories support the idea that the brain has a limited capacity for processing information and so attention has to be selective. They differ in terms of where they place the filter or bottleneck in attention processing. Broadbent places selection early on and hence it is based on the physical properties of the stimulus. Treisman's attenuation theory places the bottleneck later in processing, allowing for the possibility that the initially unattended stimulus may still be processed but on the basis of the individual's perception of it. Deutsch and Deutsch's theory places the bottleneck even later in processing, arguing that all stimuli are fully processed, with subsequent selection depending upon the perceived importance or relevance of the message they carry. Other factors contribute to the overall process of attention.

Attention spans

Attention span can be thought of as the length of time, or span, that one can pay attention to, or concentrate on one topic without becoming distracted. Learning is directly affected by our attention span and this varies with each individual.

REFLECTIVE TASK

Do you think an individual's attention span is fairly consistent or will it vary with different conditions and circumstances? Identify the factors that you think might lead to either a longer or shorter attention span.

Invariably, attention spans are quite short. One way of testing this is to stare hard at an object (e.g. a small black dot on a white background). You will be surprised how difficult this is. Attention spans vary between individuals and with age. Most children have shorter attention spans than adults and tend to be more active. This difference becomes less as the child becomes older. For a small group of children, the inability to maintain any form of sustained attention along with high levels of activity is recognised as a behavioural problem known as attention-deficit hyperactivity disorder (ADHD) and this can carry through to adulthood. Personality can also have an effect on attention span. Child (2007, p46) for instance, points out that extraverts require more breaks than introverts while performing tasks requiring concentration and cannot concentrate as consistently on repetitive tasks.

As can be seen, the length of the attention span is very much an individual matter. It is still possible, however, to make some generalisations in this area. Consider learning which is passive in nature, such as listening to a lecture. Relying largely on one sense – hearing – which is not the primary sense used in receiving information from the environment, is hard work and the capacity to maintain attention at high levels in such circumstances is limited. Typically in such a circumstance, attention span is approximately 20 minutes. Questioning can be used to make the process more interactive and so raise attention levels. Questions can be asked in a variety of ways, but if the main purpose is to engage learners and have a positive effect on attention levels, the 'four P's' technique of Pose, Pause, Pounce and Praise is usually employed and involves the following steps.

1. A general question is posed to the group as a whole, because if one learner is nominated to answer at this stage (pounce) the others will relax and 'switch off'. Posing a general question first invites the entire group to think about an answer.
2. A pause is allowed for consideration of the question. Learners are given thinking time to arrive at an answer. Teachers are given thinking time to scan the group and decide who this question is best directed towards.

3. The appropriate learner is named (pounce) and gives their answer.
4. The teacher acknowledges the answer, giving praise if appropriate and repeating the answer to the rest of the group.

If learning takes on an active form, however, such as participating in a discussion, attention spans are considerably longer although still having a finite limit. Careful monitoring of group work is required, for instance, to ensure that learners stay on task. Time limits, a specified end product and the allocation of roles such as scribe, chair or reporter can also help in maintaining attention.

Breaking up passive learning activities, such as a pure lecture, with an active learning method such as discussion will allow attention levels to be maintained for a longer period of time. Alternating methods appropriately and supporting these with a variety of different resources, in keeping with Bartlett and Burton's advice to *maintain variety of task and approach* will also keep attention levels at a reasonably high level throughout a learning session.

Divided attention

Recently, the government has introduced legislation which makes it illegal to use a mobile phone while driving. The reasoning behind this is that the brain cannot simultaneously give full attention to driving and using a mobile phone and this reduced attention to driving makes it unsafe. This is an example of divided attention.

REFLECTIVE TASK

Despite the reservations expressed above, there are many examples in life where two tasks are performed simultaneously. This is not possible for all tasks, however, and some combinations of tasks prove difficult while others are much more easily accomplished. Make a list of:

(a) combinations of tasks which you find to be impossible to perform simultaneously;

(b) combinations which are difficult;

(c) combinations which you find to be relatively easy.

For each, try to decide why this is the case and compare your thoughts with the theories you meet as you read through this next section.

Unlike focused attention studies which assume that only one stimulus can be attended to at the expense of other competing stimuli, studies of divided attention ask subjects to deliberately divide their attention and examine their ability to perform two tasks together under a variety of different conditions. Three main factors have been found to exert the greatest influence. These are:

- task similarity;
- practice;
- task difficulty.

Task similarity can be thought of in a number of ways but the most significant of these is when the similarity that exists is between the main sensory input required for each task. Most people find watching television while holding a conversation quite manageable. It is rather a different story, however, when watching television and reading a book or holding a conversation while answering the telephone. Generally, performing two tasks at once is easier when the two tasks use different senses. Tasks which both depend upon the same sense are much more difficult and in some cases almost impossible. Try, for instance, patting your head with one hand while rubbing your stomach with the other.

It is unlikely that a learner driver will want to hold a conversation or even listen to the radio while driving. Acquiring all of the various sub-skills needed to drive safely will require full attention. Experienced motorists on the other hand, can cope easily with conversations (providing they do not involve the use of a mobile phone) and enjoy listening to the radio. A number of researchers have shown that practice can have a profound effect on the ability to perform two tasks simultaneously.

Defining task difficulty is somewhat problematical as what is difficult for one person may well be easy for another. Similarly, many tasks which are difficult in the learning phase become relatively easy when mastered. The picture is further complicated by the fact that performing two tasks simultaneously may add a further layer of difficulty compared with that of perform-ing each task separately. Despite the problem of definition, a number of studies have found that increasing the difficulty of the tasks leads to a reduction in performance and, conversely, increased performance is noted when tasks are made easier.

So, it would appear that if two tasks are relatively simple, well practised and different in their sensory demands, they can be performed at the same time with relative ease. If, on the other hand, the two tasks are difficult, make demands on the same sensory channels and are only recently learned, simultaneous performance will be extremely difficult.

Theories which try to account for the simultaneous performance of tasks fall into two types.

Limited capacity approach

This theory suggests that a central processing system exists which can be used flexibly across all kinds of different tasks, but has a limited capacity or resource with which to perform this function. The number of tasks processed at one time depends upon the amount of resource each requires. If tasks are relatively easy or well practised, they will require little capacity and so can be performed at the same time. The number of tasks that can be contemplated will depend on how many of them it will take to use the total capacity of the central processor. Capacity is influenced by levels of arousal: the greater the level of arousal, the greater the processing capacity.

Multiple resource approach

Unlike the limited capacity approach, this theory suggests that several processing modules exist, each with a limited capacity, but each of which processes a different type of task. Competition for the same module leads to selection. If one task relies on sight and another on hearing, both can be simultaneously processed as each will be processed by its own particular module. If, however, both tasks are sight-dependent or both are hearing-dependent, they will be competing for the same processing module and due to limited capacity cannot be carried out simultaneously.

While it is sometimes possible to divide attention between two different tasks the mechan-ism by which this is achieved has not yet been fully explained. It certainly seems that the ability to do this can be increased by practice but even then, performance is not as good as when each task is performed alone. Divided attention will always lead to some loss in efficiency compared with focused attention. This is borne out in real life by spontaneous actions such as closing one's eyes whilst listening to music.

In a learning environment this suggests that attention distracters should be kept to a minimum and as far as possible, only one task should be performed at a time.

PRACTICAL TASK PRACTICAL TASK **PRACTICAL TASK** PRACTICAL TASK **PRACTICAL TASK**

List as many attention distracters as you can think of that might occur in a typical learning environment. Which of the senses do most of these apply to? What can be done to minimise the effect of the distracters you have identified?

Physical environment

Factors such as too much or too little light or heat can provide a distraction from the task in hand. Room arrangements which allow learners lots of eye contact or to sit in groups invite interactions which dominate attention when in terms of the learning that is to take place, it may be better focused elsewhere.

Teachers

Mannerisms are the biggest culprit here. If you are nervous, for instance, your arms and hands seem to become larger and more obvious. What do you do with them when you are not using them to help interpretation or provide emphasis? You may, perhaps, run your fingers through your hair, straighten your clothes, play with watches, rings, or loose change, or stroke your neck or forehead. All of these provide distractions that can take attention away from what is to be learned.

Resources

Visual aids can be extremely effective in capturing attention and directing it to the stimuli and information appropriate to learning. They can also act as distracters, however, and this is why whiteboards should be cleaned immediately after use and information presented visually is revealed a bit at a time.

Competing activities

Quite often, learners wish to take notes either as a memory aid or because they find that note taking helps them to process information. This, however, involves dividing attention between note taking and whatever else is taking place in the learning environment. It can help if learners are encouraged to develop methods of effective note taking, such as using abbreviations, bullet points, numbers or perhaps recording notes in the form of questions, but teachers can also make a contribution to easing the burden of note taking. Strategies revolve around either supplying the notes in the form of a handout or alternatively, providing a framework within which learners can produce their own notes, and ensuring reasonable accuracy in the notes taken as well as minimising divided attention.

It is also possible to have a direct impact on note taking through the way in which information is delivered, particularly if learners are aware in advance that strategies will be employed such as:

- visual highlighting of the main points;
- pausing after the main points;
- summarising periodically, giving a few moments to record the points made.

Summary of strategies to aid attention

Strategy	Principle
Ensure an appropriate physical and social environment	Avoid divided attention
Make objectives clear at the start of the session	Focus attention
Use a variety of activities and resources	Attention spans
Give clear, short directions before, not during an activity	Avoid divided attention
Use questions and monitor group activities	Focus attention
Use movement, gestures and voice inflection to good effect	Focus attention
Avoid distracting mannerisms	Avoid divided attention
Use 'attention pointers'	Focus attention
Devise strategies to help learners in the taking of notes	Avoid divided attention
Use the whiteboard to highlight main points. Avoid clutter	Focus attention
Use colours and images to good advantage in projection systems. Reveal only one item of information at a time	Focus attention
Clean whiteboards and close down projection systems when not directly using them	Avoid divided attention

In summary, attention is either an involuntary or voluntary process of focusing upon some signal or stimulus at the expense of others. It is the ability to actively and selectively attend to some stimuli and ignore others. Assuming learners are sufficiently motivated and interested in what is to be learned, attention is the first stage in processing that learning and so teachers need to be able to call upon a variety of strategies to both attract attention in the first place and then maintain it throughout a learning period. Attention is directly related to and overlaps with perception, which is the process of interpreting the stimuli that have been selected so they take on some kind of personal meaning.

Perception

The process of perception has already been discussed to some extent in the general view of cognitive approaches to learning presented in Chapter 4. There it was noted that rather than merely acting as passive receptors of external stimuli, we need to extract personal meaning from them. Previous experience plays an important role in achieving this as new learning builds upon existing experience and ultimately becomes part of it. The strategies which Gestalt psychology suggests we use in order to interpret incoming stimuli in a manner which imposes order and meaning, were also explored.

In this chapter, the factors which influence perception and the ways in which they affect learning are considered. Perception can be defined as:

> *The acquisition and processing of sensory information in order to see, hear, taste or feel objects in the world; also guides an organism's actions with respect to those objects.*

> (Sekuler and Blake, 2002, p621)

As previously noted, most contact with the external environment is achieved through sight and so it is in the field of visual perception that most research has taken place. Child (2007, p68) reassures us that the general principles that apply to visual perception are, however, equally applicable to perceptions involving the remaining senses of hearing, touch, taste and smell.

The role of previous experience

If past learning did not influence our perception, the curious lines on this page you are now reading, which we call letters, would not be perceived as parts of words and the words would be devoid of meaning.

(Solso et al., 2005, p75)

If you are approached by a stranger asking for directions, invariably you will start by asking them if they know where such and such a particular landmark is. You will try to find out what their existing knowledge is and use this as the basis for your explanation of how to arrive at the required destination. You are acknowledging the fact that previous experience provides a frame of reference against which incoming information can be interpreted. In the same way in which the computer compares each new word entered against all of the data it holds in its memory to check spelling, the brain compares incoming sensory information against the store of previous experience and knowledge held in memory in order to arrive at a meaningful interpretation. Previous knowledge and experience provide the starting point for perception.

Context also provides a clue as to interpretation. The word 'chip' for instance, can be interpreted in a number of different but equally valid ways. Previous experience will suggest a 'chip' could be something eaten with fish, a small piece of wood, a token used in gambling, a flaw in an otherwise perfect piece of china or a working component in a computer. If I was in a computer shop and overheard a conversation about chips I could be fairly certain as to which was the appropriate interpretation. Similarly, the middle symbol in the diagram below is capable of two different interpretations as it is presented in two different contexts. If I were to ask you which letter you thought it was, however, you would recognise the context I was referring to and give an appropriate response. This is because your perception was shaped by expectancy. The context you were given led you to expect to see a letter and so you you interpreted the figure in this light.

The advance organiser

Look back at the last sentence and read it carefully. You probably did not notice the repetition of the word *you*; you would normally expect only one *you* and so that is what you saw. Creating context or expectancy is similar to the effect achieved through the use of the 'advance organiser' proposed by Ausubel and discussed in Chapter 5. The advance organiser encourages the desired perceptual set or tendency to think along certain lines.

Ormrod (2008) distinguishes between internal organisation (the way in which the individual organises and integrates new information) and external organisation (how information is related to what is already known) and describes an advance organiser as *a general introduction to new material that is typically designed to accomplish either or both of [these] two purposes* (2008, p225). This connection is also emphasised by Bligh (2000, p86), who describes the function of an advance organiser as *to bridge the gap between what the students know already and what they need to know.* While it is often advantageous to induce perceptual set in learners in order to arrive at a common perception of what is being discussed, perceptual set can prove limiting in the context of teaching. The negative side to perceptual set is that it restricts the ability to *see matters in a different light* or think more laterally. This can result in teachers being unable to find a different way in which to explain a point that has not been understood. A possible solution can be found in asking another learner who has understood, to explain the point in their own words in the hope that their perceptual set is more accessible to the other learners.

Analogies

Another way of facilitating perception through the linking of new information to previous knowledge is through the use of analogies. As previously noted, this chapter is based around the analogy of the brain as a computer. Other commonly used analogies include the flow of electricity along a wire and the flow of water along a pipe, memory as a filing cabinet, light as water ripples or waves, the heart as a pump, fractions as slices of a cake or the Earth as acting like a greenhouse in causing global warming.

Several of the above illustrate Ormrod's assertion that analogies are most useful in cases where *the material is fairly abstract* (2008, p224). This use of analogy to simplify explanation and move from the concrete to the abstract is often adopted in everyday conversation as for instance, when referring to having a memory like a sieve or describing a problem as being the tip of the iceberg. Even W. B. Yeats resorted to the use of analogy when suggesting *Education is not the filling of a pail, but the lighting of a fire.*

In a teaching context, Woolfolk et al. (2008, p349) refer to the use of analogical instruction as *teaching new concepts by making connections with information that the pupil already understands* and claim success for the approach *for teaching scientific or cultural knowledge in heterogeneous secondary classes that include pupils who are less academically prepared and pupils with learning difficulties.*

REFLECTIVE TASK

Think of any topic that you teach which is either difficult to explain or is abstract in nature. Devise an analogy to make this particular topic easier to understand. Try it out and evaluate its success.

Like any device which is designed to simplify, however, analogies have their limitations and like elastic will only stretch so far before breaking. Analogies need to be designed with care, making sure that the relationship between the new information and the analogy is strong and reasonably self-evident. Care must also be taken in their use, the differences between the two being pointed out as well as the similarities that provide the basis for perception.

Perceptions of constancy

The world around us has the potential to provide total chaos and confusion as we perceive it. Images projected upon the retinas of our eyes from a single object vary so much that, if we depended only on data from this source, objects would have no constancy, but would appear to be different every time they were presented to us. That this does not occur is the result of perceptual constancy.

(Malim, 1994, p45)

What is this potential chaos that Malim refers to? If we always believed what we physically saw, people would appear to grow larger as they approached us, objects would change their shape and properties as we or they moved or changed position relative to each other and, under different lighting conditions, objects would appear to be a different colour. Although the above describes the images that are projected onto the retina of the eye, these images are perceived or interpreted in such a way that despite appearances, we recognise that people remain the same size, moving objects maintain their shape, and colours do not change under different lighting conditions. Perceptual constancy refers to our ability to do this. Perceptions of constancy play an important part in providing reference points for making sense of the experiences we have in the world.

Have you experienced the sensation of sitting in a car at the traffic lights looking at the car next to you and then feeling as if you are rolling backwards, grabbing for your handbrake only to find it is already on? Have you ever sat in a railway carriage, looked out of the window to see another railway carriage on the track next to yours. Your carriage moves off in a forward direction, or is it the other carriage moving off in a backwards direction? The more you look, the more difficult it is to tell which is the case. Similarly, look at the diagrams below. Is the book lying face up or face down? Is the ball at the front top right-hand corner or the back right-hand corner of the cube? Again, the more you look, the more the image 'flips' in front of your eyes.

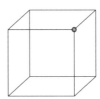

According to Gregory (1990), when we are presented by the senses with new information, we form hypotheses as to its possible meaning. More often than not, a single hypothesis stands out as the most likely interpretation and we consequently accept it. In each of the cases above, however, two equally plausible hypotheses can be formulated.

In the carriage example, hypothesis 1 is *my carriage is moving forwards* whereas hypothesis 2 states that *the other carriage is moving backwards*. When looking at the book, hypothesis 1 is *the book is lying face up* whereas hypothesis 2 is *the book is lying face down*. In each instance, as both hypotheses are equally plausible, the mind jumps from one interpretation to the other, hence our confusion.

To resolve this confusion, Gregory suggests that we seek confirmatory cues to verify one of the competing hypotheses. In the case of the railway carriage this is easily done by looking out of the opposite window. If we see that the station platform is moving, we know that this is not actually the case due to our perception of constancy relating to location. It is therefore evident that it is our carriage that is in motion. Alternatively we can turn to information from the other senses – can we feel vibrations caused by movement, can we hear the wheels of our carriage moving over the railway track? Once one of the hypotheses is confirmed through these means, we are no longer confused when looking at the other carriage. The book problem is not so easily resolved, however, as there is no confirmatory cue to support one or the other and so the mind continues to flip between one interpretation and the other.

Language

The quote at the beginning of this section on the role of previous experience refers to the written word. The most widely used form of communication in teaching and learning, however, is the spoken word. Language, or the way in which the spoken word is used, is an important factor in perception. Interpretation of the spoken word is influenced by a number of factors such as accent, dialect, register or whether the language used by the teacher is the first language of the learner. In the teaching of any subject, however, you will be introducing new terminology and using the specialised language, concepts or jargon of the subject. A sound knowledge of the terminology or jargon is an essential component of the learning that takes place within any specialist area and at some stage it has to be learned so that everyone speaks the same language. The introduction of too much specialist language on the same occasion, however, can be overwhelming and lead to learners switching off or a general lack of understanding, so a gradual introduction is normally more effective. Arriving at an understanding of the particular concept before naming it, in a manner similar to that suggested by Bruner in Chapter 5, can also be very effective. Once learned, engaging learners in activities which give them the opportunity to use the new language helps in establishing it as the norm and at the same time, provides feedback on how well it is understood.

Summary of strategies to aid perception

Strategy	Principle
Use a variety of approaches	Capture and cover all learning/perceptual styles
Encourage contributions, ideas and examples from learners	Make use of previous knowledge and experience
Use resources and hands-on approaches to full advantage	Provide plentiful auditory, visual and tactile stimuli
Give total picture first, use advance organisers and signposts	Present structure
Use plenty of analogies and examples	Build on what is already known
Ask learners to explain new concepts	Assess understanding, can be used to overcome perceptual set
Try starting from examples to introduce new terminology	Move from the concrete to the abstract
Use 'jargon' only when appropriate – introduce the concept before naming it	Use accessible language
Use problem-solving approaches	Engagement with material to be learned leads to understanding
Point out patterns in new material to be learned	Establish structure
Review learning and assist learners to identify how new learning relates to what they already know	Integrate new learning with existing knowledge and experience
Start learning sessions by reference to what has been previously learned and how it relates to what is to be learned	Establish relationships in learned material
End learning sessions by looking forward to the next session, establishing links with current learning	Establish relationships in learned material

A SUMMARY OF **KEY POINTS**

> Information processing theory is a branch of cognitive psychology which compares the brain with a computer in the way that it processes incoming stimuli.

> The analogy has its limits as a computer is a serial processor which acts in a bottom-up manner whereas the brain can also act as a parallel processor and uses a top-down approach to the processing of incoming stimulus information.

> The brain has a limited capacity. Attention prevents overloading of the brain by filtering out the vast majority of incoming stimuli. Those selected fall within the limits of the brain's processing capacity.

> Different theories suggest that filtering takes place at different stages of the process of attention.

> Some stimuli are selected on account of their physical properties while others are selected because they have some personal significance to the individual.

> Attention spans are limited, duration depending upon the type of activity engaged in. Generally attention spans are shorter in passive approaches to learning and longer when learning is active.

> Divided attention results in a loss in efficiency, particularly when tasks being performed simultaneously possess a high degree of difficulty or involve the same type of sensory input. Practice can increase the ease with which two tasks can be performed simultaneously.

> Attention distracters take many different forms in a learning environment but steps can be taken to minimise their effect.

> Perception is the process whereby learners interpret and make sense of those stimuli selected as a result of attention.

> Perception is dependent upon previous experience and so difficulties in perception arise when new material lies outside existing experience and knowledge.

> Context provides guidance to correct perceptions.

> Perception is brought about through a process of hypothesis formation and confirmation.

> Advance organisers can be used to shape learners' perceptions, and analogies provide a means of working from existing knowledge and experience.

> Perceptions of constancy allow a consistent perception of the continually changing visual environment.

REFERENCES REFERENCES **REFERENCES** REFERENCES **REFERENCES** REFERENCES

Bartlett, S and Burton, D (2007) *Introduction to education studies* (2nd edn). London: Sage.

Bligh, D (2000) *What's the use of lectures?* San Francisco: Jossey Bass.

Child, D (2007) *Psychology and the teacher* (8th edn). London: Continuum.

Francis, M and Gould, J (2009) *Achieving your PTTLS qualification: A practical guide to successful teaching in the lifelong learning sector.* London: Sage.

Gregory, RL (1990) *Eye and brain: The psychology of seeing* (4th edn). London: Weidenfeld and Nicolson.

James, W (1890) *Principles of psychology.* New York: Holt.

Malim, T (1994) *Cognitive processes.* Basingstoke: Macmillan.

Naatanen, R (1992) *Attention and brain function.* New Jersey: Lawrence Erlbaum Associates.

Ormrod, A (2008) *Human learning* (5th edn). Ohio: Pearson Prentice Hall.

Petty, G (1998) *Teaching today.* Cheltenham: Nelson Thornes.

Sekuler, R and Blake, R (2002) *Perception.* New York: McGraw Hill.

Solso, R, Maclin, M and Maclin, O (2005) *Cognitive psychology* (7th edn). Boston: Allyn and Bacon.

Woolfolk, A, Hughes, M and Walkup, V (2008) *Psychology in education.* Harlow: Pearson Education.

9
Memory and learning

Chapter overview and objectives

The ability to retain and later access the information we encounter is crucial to the process of learning. Without memory, we would not be able to draw on previous experience, seen in Chapter 8 to be essential in the performing of functions ranging from those as basic as recognising letters on a page to those as complex as decision-making. Memory provides the link between the past, the present and the future, and is a crucial stage in the process of learning. This chapter explores models of memory and their implications for practice.

When you have worked through this chapter you will be able to:

- **identify the three different processes involved in memory;**
- **differentiate between sensory memory, short-term memory, long-term memory and working memory;**
- **identify the mechanisms at work in each of the above types of memory and how these relate to the processes of memory;**
- **describe the 'levels of processing' approach to memory;**
- **recognise the importance of organisation, meaning and understanding in committing information to long-term memory;**
- **recognise that forgetting occurs for reasons of decay, displacement, retrieval failure or interference;**
- **match reasons for forgetting to different components of the memory system;**
- **describe strategies for improving memory;**
- **list the different types of mnemonic devices that might be used to assist retrieval of information from long-term memory.**

This chapter contributes to the following values and areas of professional knowledge as contained in the LLUK professional standards for teachers, tutors and trainers in the lifelong learning sector:

AS4, BS2, CS4, DS3

AK1.1, AK4.1, AK4.3, BK1.1, BK1.2, BK1.3, BK2.1, BK2.7, CK3.1

Memory processes

Memory is an information storage system and the way in which it works can be compared with another information storage system – the filing cabinet. Suppose you receive your new TV licence and wish to put it into your filing cabinet for safe keeping. The first stage in this process would be to decide what to file it under and this would depend upon how you had organised your filing cabinet in the first place. You may have organised it so that it contains files headed 'entertainment', 'household' and 'legal documents'. Under which of these categories will you file your TV licence? You decide to file it under 'entertainment' and place it into the appropriate folder to be stored until you need it again. When information is first received for storage in memory, a decision must also be made as to how and where it will be stored. This process is analogous to deciding what to file the information under and is known as encoding. Encoding normally involves changing the information into a form in which it can be subsequently stored.

To find and retrieve the TV licence from the filing cabinet, you would need to remember what you had originally filed it under. Similarly, the retrieval of stored information from memory depends upon how it was stored in the first place.

To work effectively then, memory must be capable of carrying out three processes.

- Encoding information. Information must be registered and converted to a form in which it can be stored.
- Storing information. Information is stored and is available for future use.
- Retrieving information. Information is recovered from storage when required.

A number of models of memory have been devised to explain how these processes take place and these are considered next.

Models of memory

There are a number of different views as to the exact nature of memory but in general, from an information-processing perspective, information passes through a series of stages or storage systems, each processing it in a slightly different and more refined manner until the final outcome is achieved. Atkinson and Shiffrin's multi store model of memory attempts to identify these storage systems and explain the flow of information from one to another until it is retained in its final form. This model suggests that the systems or components of memory are:

- sensory memory – large capacity, briefly stores sensory information;
- short-term memory – stores information for a longer period of time but has limited capacity;
- long-term memory – large capacity, provides a permanent store.

Ormrod (2008, p168) proposes an analogy between the way in which these systems work together and the way in which we deal with all the bits of paper collected as part of daily life. She suggests that in a typical period of time we might accumulate items such as personal letters, newspapers, bills, a driver's licence, junk mail and grocery store receipts. Junk mail and grocery receipts are discarded almost as soon as they are acquired and this is equivalent to the role of sensory memory in which items are initially registered but if considered unimportant are immediately discarded. Other items such as bills need to be dealt with briefly – they need to be paid and processed but can then be forgotten. This equates to the role of short-term memory, which stores information just long enough to use it, then discards it when it has served its function. Other items such as the driving licence, however, need to be stored away in a safe place from which they can later be retrieved when required. Information which similarly needs to be stored long term and retrieved at will progresses all the way to long-term memory. The model is represented visually below.

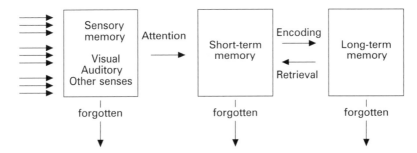

This chapter will examine each of these different components of memory and the processes by which memory functions, before exploring strategies to improve the effectiveness of memory in the learning environment.

Sensory memory

Sensory memory has been discussed in Chapter 8 as it normally precedes the attention phase of information processing. It holds a fleeting impression of incoming stimuli before either discarding them or passing them on to the next stage of short-term memory. Sensory memory takes in all of the available environmental information, creating an all-round aware-ness. Suppose you are driving your car. You are taking in all sorts of visual information related to other traffic, pedestrians, road conditions, signals, lights and auditory information relating to other traffic users, your own car's engine noises... In short, there is a vast range of sensory information which is available. Most of it becomes background, however, and you do not actually pay it specific attention. It is only when your engine splutters, a pedes-trian walks out into the road or a traffic light changes to red that it becomes the focus of your attention. In order to become the focus of attention, however, the stimulus must have been picked up in the first place and this is the function of sensory memory – to retain sensory information long enough for a decision to be made as to whether it is worth exploring further. Its capacity is therefore extremely large, but the trace left is fleeting. Stimuli are processed in their raw form, visual (iconic) information lasting for approximately half a second before fading away or being overwritten by the next incoming stimuli. Auditory (echoic) information lasts somewhat longer. The spoken word, for instance, retains a trace for between two and four seconds, essential if it is to be contextualised by the remainder of the sentence of which it is part.

Short-term memory

In the original Atkinson and Shiffrin model, short-term memory retains information for approximately 30 seconds. If you wished to memorise a telephone number only long enough to dial it, it would be stored in short-term memory but once it had served its purpose, it would be discarded rather than progress to long-term memory. It would then become forgotten. If you had to go to another part of the house to find a telephone you could use, you would maintain the number in short-term memory by repeating it to yourself until you arrived at the telephone. This process is known as rehearsal and is seen as having two functions. The first of these is to retain information in the short-term memory by renew-ing its trace. By repeating the number you can maintain it in short-term memory long enough to be able to use it. The second of these is to transfer information from short-term to long-term memory. While it is not the only mechanism by which this transfer can be achieved, Atkinson and Shiffrin regarded it as the most commonly used. If your walk to the telephone was reasonably short, the number would be forgotten once you had used it. If, on the other hand, a long walk was involved, the number may have been sufficiently rehearsed to transfer it to long-term memory. This would be an example of rote rehearsal. More effective is integrated rehearsal which is achieved *by creating a context into which the learning is embodied* (Gregory and Parry, 2006, p17).

The capacity of short-term memory is limited. Miller (1956) found that the memory span for most people was between five and nine equally weighted items and this led him to propose *the magical number seven, plus or minus two* as the limit of the capacity of short-term memory. When capacity is reached, short-term memory cannot accept any further information until further space is created either by transferring existing information to long-term memory or by losing information by forgetting.

It has been noted that when information is stored in sensory memory, it is stored in its original sensory form. On entering short-term memory, however, it is stored in a different form. The process of converting information into an appropriate form for storage is known as encoding. The exact nature of the encoding process is still a matter of some debate but it would appear to take on one of several different guises. Consider the stimulus information to be 'chair'. You could store this visually as an image, acoustically as the actual word 'chair' or you could relate it to your previous knowledge and experience of chairs you have previously encountered, in which case your chosen encoding mechanism would be semantic as the chair in question now has some personal meaning for you. Any of these encoding strategies can be used but the predominant view is that acoustic encoding seems to be the preferred method for short-term memory. This is known as rote rehearsal, whereas the establishing of meaning is known as elaborative rehearsal.

Long-term memory

Long-term memory is the relatively permanent depository of all of the memories an individual has accumulated to date. It is the most complex of the different components of the memory system and requires a great deal of organisation and flexibility in its workings in order to be able to deal with all of the different types of information and experiences it is required to store. Its exact capacity is not known but for all practical intents and purposes it can be considered as limitless. Similarly, the duration of time for which information is retained is unknown and Sternberg (2006, p166) suggests that *at present, we have no proof even that there is an absolute outer limit to how long information can be stored.*

Encoding in long-term memory can take different forms but researchers such as Baddeley (1986) suggest that semantic encoding is most widely used. This view is supported by Ormrod (2008, p183), who proposes that:

> *Another noteworthy characteristic of the knowledge in long-term memory is its* interconnectedness: *Related pieces of information tend to be associated together. Virtually every piece of information in long-term memory is probably directly or indirectly connected with every other piece.*

So, while encoding in short-term memory would involve the repetition of information (rote rehearsal), and this may ultimately also result in encoding in long-term memory, a more effective strategy for encoding information in long-term memory involves establishing some kind of relationship between the new information and existing information (elaborative rehearsal).

Working memory

Atkinson and Shiffrin's model has been subject to criticism and indeed the notion of a staged model of memory has been challenged by Craik and Lockheart (1972), who devised a 'levels of processing' model. This model suggests that all incoming information is processed by a central processor and that processing occurs at different levels of complexity. Shallow processing results in a short-lasting memory trace whereas deep processing leads to a stronger and longer-lasting trace.

Of greater impact, however, is the shift away from the concept of the relatively passive concept of short-term memory towards the more dynamic system of working memory, which is concerned not only with the temporary retention of information but also with processing and transformation of that information. Ormrod (2008, p176) describes its function as follows:

> *It identifies information in the sensory register that warrants attention, saves the information for a longer period of time, and processes it further. It may also hold and process information that it retrieves from long-term memory – information that will help in interpreting newly received environmental input.*

Sousa (2006, p45) compares working memory with *a work table, a place of limited capacity where we can build, take apart, or rework ideas for eventual storage somewhere else.*

Baddeley's (1986) original model of working memory consisted of four different components as shown in the diagram below.

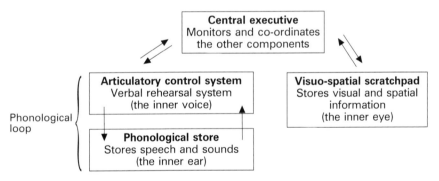

The central executive is a limited-capacity system which, like short-term memory, can deal with approximately seven items at a time. As its name suggests, the central executive controls the workings of the other components which are consequently known as slave systems. The visuo-spatial scratchpad is known as the inner eye as it is responsible for storing and when necessary, rehearsing, visual and spatial information. Baddeley (1986, p109) called it this because it was:

> *A name that was meant to suggest a system especially well adapted to the temporary storage of spatial information, much as a pad of paper might be used by someone trying for instance to work out a geometric puzzle.*

In order to emphasise the visual nature of this system he renamed it, stating his intention to *subsequently to refer to this hypothetical system as the 'visuo-spatial sketchpad'*.

Baddeley's experiments on memory had revealed that subjects were capable of manipulating and processing numbers at the same time as holding a different series of numbers in some form of short-term storage. This was at odds with the notion that working memory was merely a storage system and led Baddeley (1986, p75) to suggest:

> *One way out of this dilemma is to assume that the system involved in storing digits is not synonymous with the system involved in reasoning.*

The phonological loop is thus considered to consist of two parts – the articulatory control system and the phonological store. The articulatory control system is responsible for rehearsing acoustic or verbal information and is often referred to as 'the inner voice'. Storage of acoustic and verbal information takes place in the phonological store and is known as 'the inner ear'.

The model of working memory is constantly being re-evaluated and modified as research uncovers more information concerning memory. The existence of other systems dealing with the remaining senses has been suggested and in 2000, Baddeley suggested another component – the episodic buffer – which is capable of accessing information from long-term memory and integrating information from different parts of working memory so they take on some form of collective meaning. The central executive remains the most significant component of working memory, however, as it is here that decisions are made regarding what information is to be processed and how this is to be achieved.

Although performing a similar function to short-term memory, working memory is a much more active system and has been described by Ormrod (2008, p176) as the *consciousness of the memory system*. Working memory processes information as well as storing it and has begun to supersede short-term memory in current theorising on memory.

Organisation in long-term memory

Over a period of time, long-term memory accumulates a vast amount and variety of information. This huge bank of information needs to be organised in some way to make locating and accessing specific items of information easier.

One way in which long-term memory seeks to achieve this is by categorising information into different types and storing these in different parts of the brain. The two major types of long-term memory are declarative memory and nondeclarative memory. Declarative memory refers to memory relating to knowledge that can be stated or declared in words or symbols, and is therefore often referred to as explicit memory. It includes semantic memory (words, objects, facts, faces) and episodic memory, which is memory of events or experiences. Nondeclarative memory, or implicit memory, refers to memory relating to knowledge that cannot be explicitly stated and one example of this is classical conditioning (see Chapter 2) which is based on naturally occurring reflexes. Procedural memory – the memory involved in learning motor or cognitive skills – also comes under the heading of nondeclarative memory.

It seems that information is also grouped in memory in terms of hierarchies and meaning.

Take the information above relating to declarative and nondeclarative memory and present it in the form of a hierarchical chart. Would you find it easier to commit information to memory in this form?

In response to the reflective task above you may have produced a diagram similar to the one below.

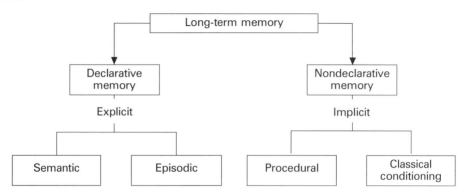

You will undoubtedly find that presented in this form, the information is easier to commit to memory than when encountered as the previous rather dense explanation. Long-term memory then, arranges and organises information as part of its encoding process, and so presenting information to be memorised in an organised fashion makes it easier to commit to memory.

REFLECTIVE TASK

Read the following three sets of information.

1. TAS – YAL – DOP – SIW – MEL – YOS – HIW – GAW – NAL – WOH – LON – MAF
2. WAS – TIN – LAY – WHY – OLD – WOE – NIL – HAM – FIG – MOP – ASS – LOW
3. WE – ALL – SAW – A – TINY – GOLDFISH – WHO – SWAM – IN – MY – POOL

Which of these is easier to commit to memory? Each set of information contains exactly the same letters. What does this tell you about memory?

The first set of information in the above task is meaningless and so the only way to commit it to memory would be through a process of rote rehearsal. You would repeat the information to yourself a sufficient number of times to transfer it to long-term memory. You would then be able to retrieve it at a later stage and repeat the sequence of letters, but it would still have no meaning as far as you are concerned. You may well have learned your 'times table' in a similar repetitive manner. The second set of information would present an easier task as it contains words that you have encountered before and therefore they have meaning for you. The easiest task of all, however, is the third set of information as the sentence itself has an overall meaning and this is fairly easily committed to memory. While meaning is personal and dependent upon previous experience, it appears to be significant in encoding information in long-term memory.

PRACTICAL TASK PRACTICAL TASK PRACTICAL TASK PRACTICAL TASK

Look at the table below for about 10 seconds, reread the passage above on meaning and then try to reproduce the table on a piece of paper.

2	9	4
7	5	3
6	1	8

There are a number of strategies that you might have employed in the above task. If, however, you realised that the table is a form of number square in which any column, row or diagonal adds up to 15, and the corners of the table present the pattern 2, 4, 6, 8, you will have undoubtedly committed the table to memory with relative ease. Understanding allows information in long-term memory to be organised in schema and therefore retrieved more easily.

Forgetting

'Forgetting' is the term that applies to the loss of information at any stage in the memory process. It can occur for a number of reasons, each of which has greater or less significance at each of the different stages of memory.

Decay refers to the tendency of a memory trace to disappear with time. If information is not selected in either sensory or short-term memory, decay is the main reason for forgetting in both of these systems. Decay can be offset in short-term memory by renewing the memory trace by means of rehearsal but in sensory memory, the trace is only fleeting and is quickly lost.

Displacement takes place when items of information have to be lost in order to make room for subsequent items. This will occur in systems with limited capacity so short-term memory is particularly prone to this type of forgetting.

The two types of forgetting described above relate to availability of information – whether or not it has been stored in the first place. Forgetting in long-term memory is largely associated with accessibility. In this instance, the memory exists but cannot be retrieved because the appropriate cue cannot be found. This is amply demonstrated in the 'tip of the tongue' phenomenon when we try to remember something that is stored in memory but we cannot find the right trigger to retrieve it. Although environmental and internal factors are thought to play a part in the effectiveness of the retrieval process, retrieval cues are closely linked to the encoding which occurs as part of the storage process and long-term memory is often referred to as cue-dependent as opposed to short-term memory, which is referred to as trace-dependent.

Interference effects form the fourth category of forgetting. These occur when competing memories or material to be remembered interfere with the process of memory. As the store of information in the long-term memory grows, for instance, it becomes more difficult to locate specific items, leading to forgetting through retrieval failure. Alternatively, competing material can prevent the transfer of information from short-term to long-term memory. If interference takes place before processing of new material, it is known as proactive interference. Retroactive interference occurs after material has been learned but prior to its recall. Interference occurs in both short-term and long-term memory and is evidenced in primacy and recency effects observed in the memorising of lists of words. The primacy effect refers to greater recall of words at the beginning of the list, whereas the recency effect refers to greater recall of words at the end of the list. Sternberg (2006, p209) explains this effect as follows:

> Words at the end of the list are subject to proactive but not to retroactive interference. Words at the beginning of the list are subject to retroactive but not to proactive interference. And words in the middle are subject to both types of interference. Hence recall would be expected to be poorest in the middle of the list. Indeed, it is the poorest.

Strategies for assisting memory

REFLECTIVE TASK

Before you read this section, make a list of the strategies you use yourself to help memory. Drawing on what you have read so far in this chapter, identify the reason for the success of each strategy.

Returning to the filing cabinet analogy, suppose you wish to retrieve a particular document. If it is a document you use a lot, then it will be a relatively simple task to locate and retrieve it. In terms of memory, information with which we are very familiar or use a lot is generally easy to retrieve. For a document you do not use on a regular basis, the ease with which you can find it will depend upon how well you organised the contents of your filing cabinet in the fist place. Are the contents organised in a logical, systematic fashion and clearly labelled or are documents placed into the filing cabinet in a fairly general and maybe even haphazard fashion? In memory, information which is stored in an organised and meaningful manner is easier to locate and retrieve. Successful retrieval strategies relate closely to those which were used to store the information in the first place.

It has already been noted that in order to store information more easily we modify or encode it in some way. The strategies we use to achieve this usually involve meaning, understanding or structuring the information in some way and are known as coding strategies. Coding strategies:

- are individual in nature, depending upon previous experience;
- involve active engagement with information;
- seek to impose meaning and achieve understanding;
- note relationships and patterns.

Effective coding leads to efficient retrieval.

PRACTICAL TASK PRACTICAL TASK **PRACTICAL TASK** PRACTICAL TASK **PRACTICAL TASK**

Turn to the list of names at the end of this chapter. Place a piece of card or paper over the list and then uncover the names one at a time. As you move down the list, dwell on each name for approximately five seconds. When you reach the bottom of the list, turn back to this page. Mentally count backwards from 20 to 1 before writing down as many of the names in the list that you can – it does not matter in which order you write them. Compare your answer with the original list.

Meaning is key to coding and humans possess a natural, spontaneous tendency to organise information into categories. What strategy did you use for the task above? Did you try to memorise the names by repeating them or did you organise them into categories of some kind? One possibility is that you grouped by occupation – politician, sportsperson, singer. Alternatively, you may have grouped according to nationality – American, British, European. This does, of course, depend upon having some prior knowledge of the individuals in the list. We often use grouping in a more deliberate manner. If you wished to memorise your shopping list for instance, you may well organise it into groups or categories such as frozen foods, vegetables, drinks.

Grouping also has the effect of reducing the number of separate items to be remembered by increasing the size of each. This strategy is known as 'chunking' and owes its significance to the assumption that short-term memory (or working memory) is of limited capacity and can only deal with approximately seven items at one time. This means, for example, that while most people can remember local phone numbers with relative ease, as they normally consist of six or seven digits, mobile phone numbers with 11 digits present a rather more difficult proposition.

Consider the following number:

07828542009

It is too long to commit to memory as a series of individual numbers. It might, however, be considered as:

078 28 54 20 09

This breaks the number up into a smaller number of 'chunks' and instead of having to remember 11 individual numbers you now have to remember five larger numbers. If the 'chunks' are familiar or can be made to have some meaning, this makes the task even easier. If the last four digits are grouped together, for instance to give:

078 28 54 2009

the last 'chunk' is easily committed to memory as it has meaning and if you happened to be aged 28 or your house number was 54, the task becomes simpler still.

Coding strategies that establish organisation and meaning in the information to be memorised allow it to be more easily encoded and stored and subsequently easier to retrieve.

REFLECTIVE TASK

Sometimes we have to learn lists of items which possess no particular meaning or logic in themselves and so coding strategies such as those described above cannot be used. Examples of such lists are the notes in the spaces of the treble clef, the planets of the solar system and the colours of the rainbow. What strategies have you come across that might help in such instances?

The kinds of coding strategies used to remember items such as those in the above task are collectively known as mnemonics. The importance of organisation and meaning in memory has been amply demonstrated and a mnemonic is a device which tries to impose some kind of artificial meaning on information in which logic or meaning do not occur naturally.

To remember the notes in the spaces in the treble clef you may have come across the mnemonic FACE, which gives the order of the notes from top to bottom. This particular type of mnemonic is known as an acronym. Other examples include ABC in First Aid training (Airway, Breathing, Circulation), which spells out the order of priorities in treating a casualty. In biology the characteristics of living things are movement, reproduction, sensitivity, growth, respiration, excretion and nutrition. The acronym MRS GREN is used to establish some meaning within this particular list.

Acronyms work on the assumption that information can be retrieved by using the first letter as a memory cue. This is not always the case. The acronym HOMES is used in geography to remember the names of the American Great Lakes. Unless Huron, Ontario, Michigan, Erie and Superior are familiar names, however, the acronym is unlikely to prompt retrieval.

It is not always possible to devise an appropriate word from the initial letters of the information to be remembered. If the notes on the lines of the treble clef were to be remembered in the same way as those between the lines, the acronym would be EGBDF – not particularly helpful as the word formed has no greater meaning or relevance than the original list of notes. In this case a sentence, *Every Good Boy Deserves Favour*, or possibly its more contemporary counterpart, *Even George Bush Drives Fast*, would be used to impart meaning. This type of mnemonic is called an acrostic and a similar strategy could be used for the planets (*My Very Easy Method Just Speeds Up Naming Planets*) or the colours of the rainbow (*Richard Of York Gave Battle In Vain*). Acrostics are often used to remember difficult spellings, as in *Rhythm Helps Your Two Hips Move*.

REFLECTIVE TASK
REFLECTIVE TASK

What strategy would you use to memorise the following list of items?
POLICEMAN   SUITCASE   APPLE   TAXI   WOODS
MOON   STRANGER   POND   HORSE   CHURCH

The list is too long to commit to memory by repetition and an acronym or acrostic would seem to be of limited use as there is no common theme in the words themselves to make them memorable, so even if a suitable acronym were constructed, would it retrieve the desired list of words? Chunking seems a better option but no meaningful groups are readily apparent. What you may well have done in this instance is to construct a story around the words. The story would have a certain logic or meaning and would contain the desired words in the correct order.

The mnemonics discussed so far work because they organise and give meaning to otherwise unrelated information. They can also chunk information, bringing it within the capacity of short-term or working memory.

A second group of mnemonics is visual in nature and relates new information to an already existing structure. The method of loci for instance, is based around a specific route or journey with which you are familiar. Objects or landmarks along the route are used to form a visual link to the items to be remembered.

Pegword systems work on a similar basis, using a sequence which is already established in memory that is used to create a visual link to new information. One example employs the following sequence:

ONE: GUN
TWO: SHOE
THREE: TREE
FOUR: DOOR
FIVE: HIVE
SIX: STICKS
SEVEN: HEAVEN
EIGHT: GATE
NINE: VINE
TEN: HEN

If the first word on the list to be memorised was 'treacle', you could form an image in your mind of a water pistol firing treacle to form a connection between the pegword 'gun' and the word to be remembered 'treacle'. Once this image had been processed, each subsequent word on the list to be memorised would be visually linked to each of the pegwords, which could be used several times over to cope with a lengthy list.

In the learning of languages, keywords provide a useful mnemonic device. The Dutch word for garden is *tuin* which is pronounced in a similar fashion to the English word *town*. To remember *tuin*, an image of an aerial view of streets with houses with gardens could be used. In this instance *town* is the keyword.

Teaching for memory

It is evident that teaching strategies that might be useful in helping learners to remember new information revolve largely, although not exclusively, around encoding and they involve repetition, organisation, meaning and understanding.

Although repetition suggests monotony, it can be achieved, while maintaining attention, through using a sequence of short but different activities all based around the same outcome or by giving a number of different kinds of tasks or exercises which involve using the same information.

You have probably come across the saying that *a picture is worth a thousand words* and in terms of memory this is often true. It can be easier to remember information which is presented visually, particularly if it also organises the information in some way. This has previously been seen to be the case with mind maps. Other examples of such graphic organisers are tables, Venn diagrams, ladders and pie charts and they are particularly useful in promoting memory because:

> they allow students to make connections among pieces of information. This makes information easier to recall. They also allow students to break information into manageable chunks. Chunking information allows students to see the relationships among the separate pieces and is key to the forming of concepts, which leads to understanding.

> (Gregory and Parry, 2006, p203)

Similarly there is an old Chinese proverb which states that

what I hear, I forget
what I see, I remember
what I do, I understand

Petty (1998, p123) quotes research which relates retention rates to different teaching approaches, varying from 5 per cent retention as a result of listening to a lecture to 90 per cent retention when making some immediate use of the learning. This concurs with Dale's cone of learning, a modified version of which (Francis and Gould, 2009, p86) is shown below.

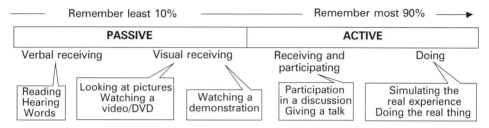

The message in all of these is clear: visual input increases retention but active engagement with the information to be remembered has an even greater effect. Exploiting closure (Chapter 3) or even using an approach based around questioning rather than explanation can be used to good effect. Any form of active learning is cognitive in nature and cognitive learning is based around meaning and understanding.

Summary of strategies to aid memory

Strategy	Principle
Present information in a structured manner	Helps learners to encode
Summarise the key points (approximately seven) at the end of a learning session	Provides structure and avoids forgetting through interference effects
Do not overload learners with information	Gives opportunity for transfer from short-term to long-term memory. Avoids forgetting through displacement
Use question and answer frequently	Practice makes the retrieval of information easier
Use mnemonics and encourage learners to devise their own mnemonics	Gives meaning to otherwise random information, thus assisting encoding of information
Use informal quizzes and short tests during learning sessions	Practice makes the retrieval of information easier
Present information in small meaningful 'chunks'	Helps encoding and eases the burden on short-term memory
Present new material at an appropriate pace – not too fast	Allows for consolidation
Use frequent summaries	Helps rehearsal and subsequent encoding
Use visual approaches, particularly those which organise information in some way	Helps encoding through chunking and understanding
Pause after important points	Gives time to process the information
Point out how new information links to previous knowledge	Helps encoding by linking new information with existing knowledge
Use activities which encourage learners to use new information	Helps with processing of information and subsequent encoding

A SUMMARY OF **KEY POINTS**

> Memory is an information storage system which operates by:
- registering and encoding incoming information;
- storing information over a period of time;
- retrieving information when required.

> The Multi Store Model of memory identifies three stages or systems of memory:
- sensory memory;
- short-term memory;
- long-term memory.

> Sensory memory has a large capacity but holds only a fleeting trace of incoming sensory information. This allows a decision to be made as to whether the information should be retained for further processing.

> Short-term memory has a limited capacity and is only capable of holding approximately seven items of information at one time. It encodes information largely through a process of repetition or rote rehearsal.

> Long-term memory is considered to be limitless in capacity and stores memories on a permanent basis. It encodes information largely through elaborative rehearsal, which establishes a relationship between new and existing information.

> The concept of short-term memory has been largely replaced by that of working memory. This is a more active system which processes information as well as storing it. It contains a central executive module which controls the operation of a number of slave systems, which deal directly with incoming sensory information.

> Information in long-term memory is organised in terms of hierarchy, meaning and understanding. This allows stored information to be more easily located and retrieved.

> Forgetting occurs when information is lost at some stage of the memory process.

> Decay refers to the disappearance of a memory trace over a period of time. Displacement occurs in limited-capacity systems when information is lost in order to make room for new incoming information. These two types of forgetting are concerned with the availability of information – whether or not it has been stored.

> Forgetting caused by the inability to retrieve information from long-term memory, due to the lack of an appropriate cue, relates to accessibility of information.

> Interference effects occur when competing memories or information cause disruption of the memory process.

> Mnemonics are used to impose meaning on otherwise meaningless information and assist the process of encoding. Mnemonics can take several different forms such as verbal (acronyms, acrostics) and visual (method of loci, pegwords, keywords).

> Visual organisers and active methods of learning increase retention.

REFERENCES REFERENCES **REFERENCES** REFERENCES **REFERENCES** REFERENCES

Baddeley, AR (1986) *Working memory*. Oxford: Clarendon Press.

Baddeley, AR (2000) The episodic buffer: A new component of working memory. *Trends in Cognitive Sciences*, 4: 417–23.

Craik, FIM and Lockhart RS (1972) Levels of processing: A framework for memory research. *Journal of Verbal Learning and Verbal Behaviour*, 11: 671–84.

Francis, M and Gould, J (2009) *Achieving your PTTLS qualification: A practical guide to successful teaching in the lifelong learning sector.* London: Sage.

Gregory, GH and Parry, T (2006) *Designing brain-compatible learning* (3rd edn). London: Corwin Press.

Miller, GA (1956) The magical number seven, plus or minus two: Some limits on our capacity for processing information. *Psychological Review*, 63: 81–97.

Ormrod, A (2008) *Human learning* (5th edn). Ohio: Pearson Prentice Hall.

Petty, G (1998) *Teaching today*. Cheltenham: Nelson Thornes.

Sousa, DA (2006) *How the brain learns* (3rd edn). London: Corwin Press.

Sternberg, RJ (2006) *Cognitive psychology* (4th edn). Belmont: Thomson Wadsworth.

Word list for practical task

1. Margaret Thatcher
2. Tiger Woods
3. George Bush
4. Charles Aznavour
5. Bobby Charlton
6. Edith Piaf
7. Michael Schumacher
8. Boris Yeltsin
9. Elvis Presley
10. Venus Williams
11. Tony Blair
12. Shirley Bassey